MASTER GRATITUDE & UNLOCK ABUNDANCE

Rewire Your Brain, Develop Gratitude Mindset, Find Peace Within, and Start Your Day With Positivity

By

DR. KALPANA GUPTA

In gratitude for all the blessings I have received and

continue to receive

Table Of Contents

"Gratitude is when memory is stored in the heart, not in the mind."

- Lionel Hampton.

Let me begin with a parable many of you might be familiar with.

A man was curious about what happened in heaven and hell. He prayed devoutly for a long time, and finally, God had pity on him and decided to show him the two places. God took him first to hell. Here, there was a vast banquet table overflowing with delicious food. The strange part was that the people sitting around the table were emaciated, miserable, and famished.

He was surprised and expressed it.

"Look carefully, "the Lord told him.

Looking closely, he noticed these people had long spoons fastened to their arms. The spoons were so lengthy that they could not bring the food to their mouths.

He was next taken to heaven. Again, he saw a similar scene: delicious food served at the banquet table and long spoons attached to the arms of people sitting around. However, the people at this table were well-fed and happy. What was different was that they were not struggling to feed themselves. Instead, they used the long spoons to feed each other.

We don't need to die to reach heaven or hell. These two places are accessible while we are alive in the world. In hell, people focus solely on themselves, ignoring the plight of others. The consequence is suffering. In heaven, people care for one another and are thankful for each other's support. Happiness naturally follows as a consequence.

"If you concentrate on finding whatever is good in every situation, you will discover that your life will suddenly be filled with gratitude, a feeling that nurtures the soul."

— *Rabbi Harold Kushner.*

We are all energy beings. Our frequency differs depending on whether we think and act negatively or positively.

Einstein proved that "everything in the world is energy," encompassing both the animate (the animal and plant kingdoms) and the inanimate (the material things in the world). We are part of this energy spectrum, each of us vibrating at a particular frequency. The energy frequency we vibrate at will be low if fear, shame, guilt, anger, and similar emotions dominate. Conversely, love, joy, peace, and gratitude elevate our energy frequency to the highest levels.

So, why do we want to maintain a high frequency? A high frequency attracts positive people, events, and things into our lives, drawing us closer to the superconscious. We can refer to this as God or the Universe.

Conversely, the low frequency of ingratitude will bring us down even more. I want to own a luxurious house, yet I keep complaining about my current one. Getting the new house becomes even more difficult because I am not grateful for what I already have.

The energy frequency I emit when I feel ungrateful attracts a life filled with more reasons to feel ungrateful. When I am weighed down by negative emotions that lower my frequency, whether anger, dissatisfaction, jealousy, resentment, or fear, I block my path to the good life I seek.

"Be thankful for what you have; you'll end up having more. If you concentrate on what you don't have, you will never have enough."

– Oprah Winfrey.

Writing this book is not merely an intellectual exercise for me; it involves much more. I am incredibly grateful to my friend Ravi Tewari for suggesting this topic and for his immense help navigating the technical and publishing aspects.

Researching and writing it has been a profound experience, bringing me serenity and contentment for all I have been blessed with. I am learning to accept whatever happens in my life, whether good or bad, with gratitude. At times, it can be challenging to embrace tough situations.

During these moments, gratitude serves as my anchor, rescuing me from dwelling on and suffering in the turbulent waters of painful experiences, doubt, resentment, depression, anxiety, ill health, and negative thoughts.

The average person's mind, including mine, often focuses on the potential problems when trying something new. The defensive or threat-response part of our brain considers and reacts to what could go wrong. In highly challenging moments, it can interfere with our ability to reason and find solutions, even as it tries to keep us safe and away from harm.

The threat-response circuits are more robust, as they are the default networks. We need to practice activating our gratitude and decision-making circuits regularly.

Over time, these circuits will become dominant, leading to happier, more productive, and more fulfilling lives.

"Being thankful is not always experienced as a natural state of existence, we must work at it, akin to a type of strength training for the heart."

– Larissa Gomez.

I invite you to join me in exploring the depth of this complex emotion, gratitude. I am confident that you will discover, as I did, that this path leads to joy and fulfilment.

CHAPTER 1

WHY PRACTICE GRATITUDE

"I live in the space of thankfulness — and for that, I have been rewarded a million times over. I started giving thanks for small things, and the more thankful I became, my bounty increased. That's because — for sure — what you focus on expands. When you focus on the goodness in life, you create more of it."

— Oprah Winfrey

THE ESSENCE OF GRATITUDE

You might say, "I am a very grateful person. I have thanked you for what you did for me."

My response would be, "That is a superficial level of gratitude. You thanked me solely because I expected to receive thanks for what I did for you. Tell me, do you ever feel truly thankful from the heart for anything you receive, whether frequently or even occasionally?"

"What does the heart have to do with it?"

"Going deeper into the feeling can transform your life and bring you joy."

You are intrigued now. "Really? Tell me more about this concept."

Dear reader, welcome to an in-depth exploration of gratitude. We tend to grasp gratitude intuitively. However, defining it in formal terms proves elusive. Is it an emotion, a character trait, or a behavioural pattern?

How does one define gratitude?

Gratitude originates from the Latin word "gratis," which means "thankful" or "pleasing." It encompasses a sense of appreciation for acts of kindness and acknowledging what we have. This complex emotion can transform people's lives and bring them happiness.

If you have read books or articles on gratitude before picking up this book, you likely encountered the name of Brother David Steindl-Rast, a Benedictine monk known as the 'Grandfather of Gratitude. 'At 98 years of age, he continues to spread his message about gratefulness as the true source of lasting happiness. He asserts, "Two things must come together for someone to feel gratitude: First, we must experience something we enjoy, and secondly, it must be a gift.

In other words, it should be free—we haven't purchased it, traded for it, or earned it. When these two conditions are met, joy arises spontaneously."

Speaking of spontaneous joy, I remember the **story of a poor boy without shoes**.

The weather was freezing cold. The marketplace quickly emptied as snow began to fall, and shoppers hurried back to their warm homes. A poor boy walked slowly, seemingly impervious to the cold.

The shoe shop owner watched him curiously, wondering if he felt the cold. But yes, he did feel cold. He shuffled into the shoe shop as the snow started to fall harder. There he stood, shivering just inside the doorway.

The owner noticed his bare feet and asked, "What happened to your shoes?"

"They were torn, sir, so I couldn't wear them."

The owner smiled kindly at him and invited him to sit down. Then, he entered the shop and returned with a new pair of shoes. He helped the boy put them on and ensured that they were comfortable.

The poor boy gazed at him, awestruck, asking, "Are you God?"

"No son, I am his servant."

The boy was filled with pure joy as he laughed. He no longer felt the cold and joyfully ran outside. Then, he looked up at the sky and whispered, "God, I just met one of your angels."

You may have also come across the name of Robert Emmons, an American psychologist and professor at the University of California, Davis, who is well-known for his research on gratitude. He says that gratitude involves both a giver and a receiver. The giver can be another person, an animal, God, a supernatural being, or a higher power. Love, compassion, or generosity may motivate the freely given gift. The receiver has not earned it, is not entitled to the gift received, and must recognize it as something good, freely given without transactional expectations. Emmons identifies two essential steps in the gratitude process: recognizing that one has received a positive outcome and acknowledging that the source of this goodness is external.

A crucial point about gratitude is that it must come from someone else. You cannot be grateful to yourself. For instance, if you ordered a sumptuous meal and enjoyed it, you cannot say that you are thankful to yourself for that lovely meal. Yes, you can express gratitude to whomever you look up to—the Universe, God, Allah, Krishna... for the good you are experiencing.

It has been said that gratitude and happiness are closely intertwined in cause and effect.

Br. David Steindl-Rast explores the relationship between them. Many people assume that when they are happy, they will experience gratitude. But is that truly the case?

Many people have everything they need, yet they are unhappy.

Why?

Because once they have obtained what they once coveted, they desire something different or want more of what they already possess.

Some people have faced misfortune yet remain genuinely happy.

Why?

They are grateful for what they have despite facing an adverse situation.

Thus, it is gratitude that brings us happiness rather than the other way around.

Summer Allen from the University of California speculates about the biological roots of gratitude in his paper, *The Science of Gratitude*. He suggests that gratitude could have significantly influenced human evolution. Selfless generosity toward others reciprocated in turn—namely, reciprocal altruism—may have served as a stepping stone to cooperation and helped forge strong social bonds. In this manner, people learned to live together, allowing societies to develop and progress.

The different levels of gratitude

There are various levels of gratitude on a continuum, ranging from the simple habit of saying thank you to a profound, sustained sense of gratefulness for life itself. At the deep end of this spectrum, a grateful person embraces all of life—good and bad. Everything that happens is perceived as a gift or, at times, as an opportunity arising from a challenging situation. Where would you place yourself on this spectrum? I know that I used to be at the superficial level before I began researching gratitude and realized its depth and what it entails.

The ***tale of two travellers*** visiting a village will further clarify the mindset concept.

A weary traveller arrived at a village. He saw an old farmer working in his field and asked, "What are the people like who live here?"

The farmer inquired, "What type of people did you encounter in the last village you visited?"

The traveller said with disgust, "Very bad. They were unkind and unhelpful. How are the people in this village?"

The farmer replied, "You will find the same kind of people here."

Sometime later, another traveller arrived in the village and spoke with the farmer to inquire about the villagers.

"What were the people like in the last place you visited?" asked the farmer.

"They were very kind and helpful. I will never forget them," the traveller replied.

The farmer said, "Well, that's exactly the kind of people you'll find here."

The first traveller had a negative mindset, exaggerating minor problems and blaming others.

The second traveller maintained a positive mindset, overlooking minor issues and focusing on the positive aspects.

Which mindset would you prefer, that of the first traveller or the second?

We can also distinguish between thankfulness and a deeper understanding of gratitude to delineate the various levels of gratitude. Gratitude possesses an essence that thankfulness lacks, as thankfulness is a transient emotion linked to a benefit received.

Thankfulness is transactional, while gratitude is a profound emotion. For example, imagine walking down the road with a stack of books. As you step onto the pavement, the books tumble and scatter everywhere. A nearby person helps you gather them, and you thank him. He expects your gratitude for his assistance, and you fulfil that expectation. The transaction is complete, and you continue without further emotion. However, if this person goes above and beyond by carrying your books to your destination, it becomes a gift you hadn't earned.

You didn't anticipate him going out of his way to help you. It's only natural to feel deeply grateful and express that sentiment. This interaction creates lasting happiness for both the giver and the receiver, making it more likely that you will want to help others. Gratitude allows individuals to experience joy and motivates them to spread kindness to others.

"Thankfulness is the beginning of gratitude. Gratitude is the completion of thankfulness. Thankfulness may consist merely of words. Gratitude is shown in acts."

– Henri Frederic Amiel

Our holy scriptures extol us to be grateful for what we have and to be thankful to our parents, teachers, and God for his abundance.

A passage appears in several Gospels in the **Bible** (the Gospel of Matthew, the Gospel of Luke, and the Gospel of Mark), specifically from the teachings of **Jesus Christ** in the New Testament:

"Whoever has will be given more, and he will have an abundance. Whoever does not have, even what he has, will be taken from him."

If read casually, this passage suggests that the wealthy will grow more prosperous while the poor will become poorer.

However, after many centuries, the mystery has been unravelled by the unveiling of hidden words in the passage: Faith, Gratitude, and Wisdom.

After this revelation, the passage is understood as follows:

Those who cultivate gratitude, faith, and wisdom will receive even more incredible blessings. Conversely, those who neglect their spiritual gifts will forfeit whatever little they possess.

In the Hindu Religious text, the **Bhagavad Gita** (18.62), **Lord Krishna**, while teaching Arjuna on the battlefield of Kurukshetra, tells him:

"tam eva śharaṇam gachchha sarva-bhāvena bhārata tat-prasādāt parāṁ śhāntim sthānam prāpsyasi śhāśhvatam"

This verse is interpreted as encouraging gratitude and surrender to the divine, emphasizing that true peace and eternal bliss come through divine grace.

Now, let's explore gratitude more intensely. Is there a connection between gratitude and happiness, or is it merely hype?

GRATITUDE AND HAPPINESS

There has been a growing awareness of the importance of practising gratitude to enhance happiness and promote good physical health in individuals and society. Interest in this vital emotion has been rekindled in recent years, although the concept is quite ancient, tracing back to the Stoic philosophers around 300 BC. The Stoics believed we should be grateful for all the people and events that shape our lives. We shouldn't only be thankful for the gifts we receive and our relationships with friends and family but also acknowledge and appreciate the challenges we encounter.

A story about a businessman and a farmer

A businessman had accumulated wealth and had every convenience at his disposal. Whenever a new model of any convenience was released, he acquired it, believing it would bring him happiness. However, his joy faded after a few days, and he soon became dissatisfied again.

Once, he travelled in his new car to the city outskirts to see how fast it could go. He was intrigued by an unmelodious yet joyful song coming from the field across the road. He asked his driver to stop the car and stepped out. A farmer was singing loudly on a cot outside his ramshackle cottage.

As the businessman approached, he realized that the farmer was impoverished.

He asked, "Are you happy?"

"Of course, I'm happy," the farmer replied.

The businessman could not believe it. "How can you be happier than I am when you have so little?"

The farmer smiled, "I am in tune with nature. The sky is my roof. The sun wakes me in the morning with cheerful light and birdsong; the stars lull me to sleep at night. My family loves me, and I have enough food to eat. Why shouldn't I be happy? I'm rich because I'm grateful for and content with what I have."

Gratitude is not just about saying "thank you." It represents a mindset and emotional state that influences how individuals view their lives and circumstances. Adopting a gratitude mindset can greatly enhance enjoyment and overall well-being.

You may wonder if that means that you can't be happy, especially since you experience many anxious moments. Let me assure you, dear reader, that anxiety does not exclude happiness.

Being grateful does not mean one is free from anxiety. Anxiety is not an optional emotion; it is an integral part of life. We begin our life journey with anxiety. Consider this: the baby in the mother's womb is suddenly pushed out.

The baby, entirely dependent on the mother for all its needs, now faces a tremendous struggle during birth. The first thing a newborn does is cry because, to survive, one must activate the lungs to breathe. Although we do not remember this anxious time, we can reflect on it and recognize that we survived that turbulent event and came into existence.

We live in a world where we require concrete evidence for everything. So, is there any solid proof that practising gratitude leads to happiness? Yes, there is. To satisfy your curiosity, I will share a few scientific studies with you.

The Scientific Confirmation of the Connection between Gratitude and Happiness

Scientific research confirms that gratitude and happiness are intertwined

Research conducted in recent years has shown that practising gratitude strengthens specific neural networks in our brains, which enhances happiness and reduces threat perceptions. Numerous studies demonstrate that appreciation positively impacts both mental and physical health. A few of these studies are as follows:

Dr. Robert A. Emmons is renowned for his extensive research on gratitude. In 2003, he conducted a study to explore the connection between gratitude and happiness.

The results indicated that participants who kept a gratitude journal reported higher levels of well-being, improved physical health, and greater optimism than those who focused on problems or neutral events.

In 2017, researchers Fuschia M. Sirois and Alex M. Wood conducted a longitudinal study at the University of Sheffield to explore the relationship between gratitude and depression in individuals with chronic illnesses.

This research demonstrated that higher levels of gratitude are linked to lower levels of depression over time in individuals with chronic conditions such as arthritis and inflammatory bowel disease (IBD).

Priyanka and Prof. Sandeep Singh conducted a systematic review in 2023 to explore the connection between gratitude and well-being. The review highlighted that gratitude is associated with increased happiness, better mental health, and improved physical health.

Neuroscience further supports the link between gratitude and happiness. Studies using functional magnetic resonance imaging (fMRI) reveal that expressing gratitude stimulates brain areas associated with reward, social bonding, and stress relief.

Okay, so you've acknowledged that gratitude and happiness are connected. But how does it work?

How Does Gratitude Enhance Happiness?

We can identify several methods through which this can happen:

Shifting focus from scarcity to abundance.

Gratitude encourages individuals to focus on what they have rather than their lack. A grateful attitude leads to an appreciation for the present moment and the blessings in one's life.

Strengthening relationships

Expressing gratitude strengthens social bonds. When people acknowledge and appreciate the kindness of others, relationships are enriched, fostering deeper connections.

Reducing stress and negative feelings

Gratitude alleviates stress, anxiety, and depression by redirecting focus from negative emotions. Grateful individuals may discover opportunities even in challenging situations, which increase their emotional resilience and allow them to cope more effectively with adversity.

So much for praising gratitude. What about the opposite emotion – ingratitude- and what issues can it cause in our lives?

THE COST OF INGRATITUDE

A proud man is always looking down on things and people, and, of course, as long as you are looking down, you cannot see something that is above you.

--C. S. Lewis

"I said thank you, didn't I? Then why do you call me ungrateful?" James argued with his office team members.

Your offhand 'thank you' feels like you're tossing scraps to birds. We don't feel appreciated for the risks we took to help you. You act as if you're entitled to our help, which leads us to question why we ever offered it.

What does ingratitude include? It is the failure to recognize and appreciate the good in our lives. Resentment, bitterness, jealousy, discontent, self-pity, and a sense of entitlement can create dissatisfaction and unhappiness, making it difficult for individuals to find joy and fulfilment.

Philip C. Watkins highlights several inhibitors of gratitude in his treatise, 'Gratitude and the Good Life.' According to him, people have four traits that inhibit gratitude: suspiciousness, indebtedness, envy, and narcissism. He rates narcissism as the most significant inhibitor.

Narcissists have an inflated ego and feel entitled to everything others do for them. They expect more from everyone, which creates strained relationships.

The effects of ingratitude influence every aspect of life, leading to emotional, physical, and relational difficulties.

There's a ***classic story about ingratitude*** that goes like this:

A software expert headed to an institution hub for an important meeting with prospective clients. He was stymied when he reached the parking area—it was packed. He made another two rounds, hoping to find a place, but he couldn't. Now, he was getting late for the meeting. Desperate, he prayed fervently, "Dear God, please let me find a place to park now. I need it very badly. Please, God, help."

A man got into a parked car and drove away right in front of his car. The expert said quickly, "I got my parking, God. You needn't bother yourself."

Let us examine in more detail the effects of ingratitude on various aspects of life and how it affects the quality of life.

Emotional and psychological effects

Ingratitude profoundly affects our emotional and psychological health. Some people tend to focus excessively on what they lack instead of appreciating what they have, negatively comparing themselves to those with more.

This unfavourable comparison may involve material possessions, careers, health, or relationships. Feelings of inadequacy and frustration can become familiar, raising their stress levels and anxiety. This negative mindset can create a self-perpetuating cycle, where dwelling on unmet desires results in increased stress and anxiety.

Feelings of inferiority will arise if one consistently compares oneself negatively to others. Focusing on perceived shortcomings instead of recognizing strengths and accomplishments results in low self-esteem.

In addition, ingratitude can contribute to depression. Not appreciating life's positive aspects may make individuals feel disconnected and resentful, creating a sense of hopelessness. Over time, this increases the risk of depression.

Physical health effects

Chronic stress from negative emotions can lead to various physical health issues in addition to psychological effects. Prolonged elevated levels of the stress hormone cortisol contribute to widespread harmful impacts on the body. Common issues include cardiovascular problems, a weakened immune system, and gastrointestinal disorders.

Chronic stress can lead to cardiovascular issues, including high blood pressure, angina, heart attacks, and stroke.

Ongoing negative emotions and persistent stress lead to a weakened immune system. These individuals are more susceptible to infections and chronic illnesses.

People holding onto resentment and dissatisfaction often struggle to relax, disrupting sleep. In turn, poor sleep quality exacerbates mental and physical health problems.

Ineffective coping mechanisms can drive individuals experiencing negative emotions to turn to alcohol or drugs. Substance abuse and addiction have far-reaching consequences that affect every aspect of life – physical health, mental well-being, relationships, and career advancement.

Effect on relationships

Failure to appreciate and acknowledge the efforts and kindness of others weakens relationships. Ungrateful individuals often take loved ones for granted, feeling entitled to their goodwill and forbearance. Over time, this lack of appreciation can lead to strained relationships. Family members, friends, and colleagues may feel overlooked and undervalued. As a result personal and professional relationships suffer.

While gratitude encourages generosity and reciprocity, ingratitude leads to isolation and diminished social support. Over time, a reputation for being ungrateful can drive others away, leaving the individual feeling lonely and disconnected.

A tale of the ungrateful son

An older man lived with his son's family after his wife passed away. He felt lonely and unwanted, as his son often ignored him. His son and daughter-in-law frequently went out for meals, leaving the father to make do with leftovers from previous dinners. One day, the son intended to take his wife and their 5-year-old son to a newly opened restaurant that was quite far away. However, he did not want to bring his father along. So, what could be done about him? That day, there were no leftovers available either.

He discussed the issue with his wife, who offered him an idea. As his family prepared to leave, he told his father, "We have to go out now, Father. However, there is no leftover food available today. Do you remember the temple nearby? They serve free meals to anyone around 1 p.m. So, you can go there to eat today." After saying this, the son went out with his family.

On the way to the restaurant, the 5-year-old son was thoughtful and quiet. When asked why he was so silent, he replied, "I will also stay in a house near a temple when I grow up."

"But why?"

"So that when I go out, you can go there for food," his son replied.

Now, realization dawned on the son. His father had given him everything within his capacity when he was young, just as he is doing now for his son. His father was stingy with himself so that he could provide the best of everything to his son. But instead of looking after his father's needs when he needed help, he ignored him. How would he feel if his son treated him like that?

He informed his wife and son that they would all return home. He suggested that they purchase something that could be packed and brought back so they could enjoy eating together.

From then on, the son treated his father kindly and ensured he received the best of everything.

Effects on career

Employees not appreciating their work, colleagues, or career opportunities often experience low motivation and decreased performance. In contrast, those who cultivate gratitude usually enjoy higher morale and productivity.

Employees who express appreciation for their colleagues and supervisors develop strong workplace relationships and build robust professional networks.

On the other hand, individuals who show ingratitude may face difficulties in workplace relationships, hindering their career development and progress.

Philosophical Implications

Ungrateful individuals who do not appreciate others or life find their existence meaningless. They constantly seek validation from others or chase material possessions to fill the void.

These individuals show low resilience during challenging times. We all know that life is not a smooth journey; thus, hardships are unavoidable. Grateful people find hope and opportunity even in difficult moments, while ungrateful individuals feel powerless and despondent.

Therefore, understanding our weaknesses and seeking solutions becomes increasingly important. Recognizing the consequences of ingratitude motivates us to cultivate gratitude and appreciation every day.

Gratitude is not a trivial ritual for the naïve. Over the last two decades, much emphasis has been placed on its effects. Scientific research has demonstrated that genuine gratitude can create magic. The next chapter will explore more of what science reveals about gratitude.

- **Gratitude is a freely given gift.** The process of gratitude involves two steps. First, we acknowledge the gift we have received, which is given freely without any transactional expectations. Second, the gift must come from someone other than ourselves; we cannot be grateful to ourselves.

- **Gratitude Enhances Happiness and Well-being -** Gratitude is not merely about expressing "thank you"; it represents a mindset that shapes how individuals perceive their lives, fostering contentment and enhancing overall well-being.

- **Scientific evidence links gratitude to happiness.** Studies confirm that gratitude strengthens the neural networks associated with happiness, reduces stress, and enhances mental and physical health.

- **Gratitude Shifts Focus from Scarcity to Abundance -** By focusing on what one has rather than what is lacking, gratitude fosters an appreciation for the present moment and life's blessings.

- **Gratitude Strengthens Relationships and Lowers Stress -** Expressing gratitude improves social bonds and fosters deeper connections while helping individuals manage stress, anxiety, and adversity.

- **Ingratitude Leads to Emotional and Psychological Distress -** Focusing on what one lacks instead of appreciating what one has can lead to stress, anxiety, and dissatisfaction. Persistent unfavourable comparisons contribute to low self-esteem and an increased risk of depression.

- **Ingratitude Negatively Impacts Physical Health** - Chronic stress due to ungratefulness can raise cortisol levels, resulting in cardiovascular issues, weakened immunity, and poor sleep quality. Extreme stress can also result in substance abuse and addiction as coping mechanisms.

- **Damages Personal and Professional Relationships** - Failing to appreciate the efforts of others can strain relationships, making family, friends, and colleagues feel undervalued. Over time, this lack of gratitude isolates individuals and weakens social bonds.

- **Ingratitude Hinders Career Growth** - Employees who fail to appreciate their work and colleagues suffer from low motivation and weak workplace relationships, which can slow career progress. Conversely, gratitude fosters a more productive and positive work environment.

CHAPTER 2

THE SCIENCE BEHIND GRATITUDE

Our brains are plastic, and we can change and shape them throughout our entire lives

- Andrew Huberman

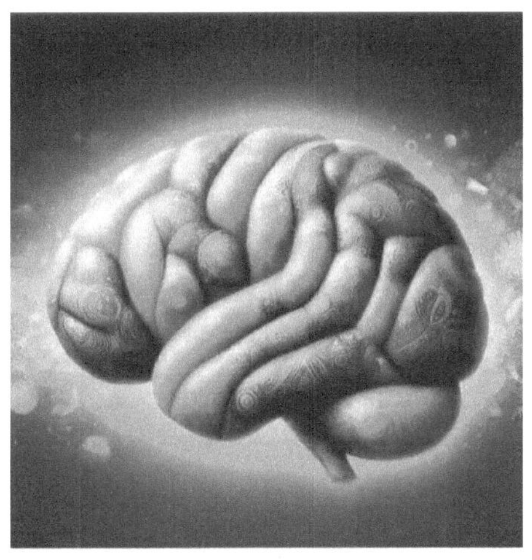

REWIRING OF THE BRAIN BY GRATITUDE

How gratitude rewires the brain for positivity

Are you wondering whether I've lost it? How can just being grateful rewire the brain? Yes, it's true. Read on, and you will understand what goes on in our brains.

Gratitude is fundamentally a social emotion. It is recognized as prosocial behaviour that reflects a mindset encouraging more active engagement with others and ourselves. Consequently, prosocial behaviour benefits individuals and society through cooperation, assistance and sharing.

Our brain houses numerous neural circuits for various functions. The circuit associated with gratitude and prosocial behaviour is regulated by a region known as the Medial Prefrontal Cortex (MPFC).

This area, crucial for decision-making and generosity, is essential in processing gratitude. Situated deep within the frontal lobe, it acts as a switch to activate the neural circuits that support gratitude and decision-making while downregulating circuits linked to threat responses or defensive behaviours, which are mediated by the amygdala.

Certain neuromodulators activate the MPFC. Neuromodulators are released in one area of the brain and act on other brain areas and neural circuits. The main neuromodulators associated with gratitude are serotonin, oxytocin, and dopamine, with serotonin being the most important.

In case you are wondering what I mean by prosocial behaviour, let me give you an example of prosocial behaviour with this story:

Paid in Full with a Glass of Milk

A poor boy went door to door to sell goods to pay his school fees. He hadn't sold much stuff, and he was hungry and exhausted. He thought of asking for food from the people in the next house on his round.

When he knocked on the door, it was opened by a young woman. His courage failed him, and he requested a glass of water instead of food.

The kind woman could make out that he was hungry. She brought him a large glass of milk. As he drank the milk slowly, he felt grateful and energized again.

He asked her, "How much do I owe you?"

She refused to take anything, "You don't owe me anything. Mother has taught us never to accept payment for kindness."

The boy thanked her from his heart and continued his round of selling; his faith in God and the goodness of humankind rekindled.

Many years passed. The young woman became critically ill. Since local doctors could not help her, she was sent to a big hospital in the city. Dr. Howard Kelly was one of the specialists who studied her case. When he saw her, he recognized her immediately and determined to cure her.

He used all resources at hand to research and cure her illness. It was a long struggle, but finally, Dr. Kelly succeeded in curing her.

When the hospital bill was given to her, the woman was afraid to open and look at it. She thought that it would take the rest of her life to pay for it. Finally, when she gathered courage and opened it, something written in a corner of the bill caught her eye. It read....

Paid in full with one glass of milk

Signed by Dr. Howard Kelly

Tears flowed from her eyes as joy and gratitude filled her heart.

So, in this story, who was giving selfless service to whom? When we consider the situation, both the young woman and Dr. Kelly practised prosocial behaviour—kindness towards another person without expectations.

The Positive Psychology Movement

Many of you may recall that until the late twentieth century, when someone said they were psychologists, the immediate response was, "Oh, oh! You are dealing with panic, depression, and so forth."

Dr. Andrew Huberman from Stanford University School of Medicine discusses the psychology of mindset in the last century, highlighting the emotions of unhappiness, anxiety, depression, and pessimism, which are controlled by defensive neural circuits. Subsequently, the positive psychology movement emerged, studying the prosocial neural circuits that contribute to positive feelings such as happiness, love, care, and generosity.

Huberman explains that the opposing neural circuits—prosocial and defensive—function like a metaphorical seesaw. He suggests that there is likely an asymmetry in their design that favours the defensive circuits. This reasoning is logical, as the defensive circuits are intended to keep us safe in various ways and would be more dominant.

Therefore, developing a gratitude practice and actively engaging with it is essential to foster feelings of well-being and happiness. A gratitude mindset activates the MPFC, which is associated with prosocial behaviour while inhibiting the amygdala, which is responsible for the threat response. As a result, it affects experiences, and the ensuing thoughts and actions lead to significant health benefits.

Moreover, the benefits of gratitude practices are lasting; they remain with us. The prosocial neural pathway becomes more pronounced when engaging in regular gratitude practice. Over time, this results in greater happiness, even when one is not actively practising gratitude.

Expressing and Acknowledging Gratitude

Huberman cites data indicating that the most effective form of gratitude practice involves not just giving or expressing gratitude but also receiving appreciation and thanks.

However, waiting for someone to thank us for experiencing the positive effects of gratitude is impractical. Similar benefits can be derived from recalling a powerful story about gratitude or observing another person receive heartfelt appreciation for a crucial service or item.

Neuroscientist Dr. Glenn Fox from USC's Brain Imaging Centre also discusses how these neural networks can be made robust. The most compelling stories of gratitude come from Holocaust survivors who survived with the help of others.

The Shoah Foundation Institute houses the world's largest archive of videotaped testimonies from Holocaust survivors.

Many survivors recounted their experiences of receiving life-saving assistance and expressed deep gratitude for the support provided. Researchers measured brain activity in subjects watching the videos using fMRI and found that prosocial networks displayed significantly increased activity during this process.

Furthermore, the activity level in the medial prefrontal cortex (MPFC) corresponded with the level of gratitude experienced. Thus, the intensity of appreciation felt correlates with MPFC activity.

Therefore, gratitude must be genuine, whether it is given or received. The positivity it contributes to our system correlates with the degree of gratitude felt.

Neuroplasticity

What we have discussed above is neuroplasticity, the brain's ability to form and reorganize neural pathways. Like muscles, the brain follows the 'use it or lose it' principle. Over time, frequently used neural pathways become more robust. Regular gratitude practice strengthens the prosocial circuits while inhibiting the defensive ones.

Consequently, these individuals become more resilient and are better able to see opportunities for growth hidden in the challenges they encounter.

Due to positive neuroplasticity, consistent gratitude practice offers numerous psychological and emotional benefits. The following section focuses on these benefits.

The Story of John D. Rockefeller

John D. Rockefeller is recognized as the world's first billionaire and a philanthropist whose generosity inspired many. However, he was not initially a philanthropist. In his early years, Rockefeller aimed to accumulate more and more wealth. By the age of 53, he had achieved his dream of being one of the wealthiest men in the world. Nevertheless, his wealth did not bring him happiness or health. Instead, he experienced unhappiness due to extreme stress, sleep disturbances, and various physical health issues. His doctors warned him that if he continued his current lifestyle, he would not live much longer.

He realized that his hoarded wealth was useless if it remained solely with him. It could not bring him happiness, nor could it benefit anyone else. Instead of being obsessed with making money, he redirected his focus to philanthropy. He committed himself to helping people and giving back to society. Rockefeller founded several charitable organizations, including the Rockefeller Foundation, established in 1913, which focuses on public health, medical training, and research. Its mission is to promote the well-being of humanity throughout the world.

As philanthropy, gratitude, and a strong belief in God became ingrained, Rockefeller's life and health began to transform. He found happiness and fulfilment, along with good health. He lived to the age of 98, more than 40 years after it was speculated that he would die any day.

He gave generously and received the appreciation of the countless individuals he assisted, which illustrates the significance of gratitude and generosity.

The most important aspect of gratitude is that instead of concentrating on what is missing in our lives, we focus on what we have. What are the psychological benefits of this emotion? Let's explore them:

Stress Reduction

If our minds seek something to worry about, there is no shortage of anxiety-inducing issues. A grateful person focuses on the abundance we are blessed with, not on what is lacking. Feeling gratitude for what we have activates the prosocial neural circuits in our brains, promotes happiness, and reduces stress.

The Incidence of Depression Decreases.

When individuals with chronic illnesses practice gratitude, they often feel more peaceful and accepting of their conditions. In 2017, F. M. Sirois and A. M. Wood from the University of Sheffield researched this concept.

They conducted a longitudinal study to identify any correlation between gratitude and depression among chronically ill individuals. Their focus was specifically on those suffering from arthritis and inflammatory bowel disease.

The study revealed that over time, gratitude was a significant predictor of lower levels of depression in these individuals.

Resilience when facing challenges

As we navigate life's journey, we encounter joyful and sorrowful moments. Challenges and obstacles persist along the way. Gratitude enables us to focus on what we have. For instance, when someone experiences a business loss and feels devastated, the best course of action is to try to reframe that traumatic experience and seek solutions. A practical approach is to concentrate on positive aspects and count blessings. For example, one can appreciate the support from family and friends, the food enjoyed daily, the roof over one's head, access to clean drinking water, and the vehicle that takes us where we need to go. Grateful individuals are less likely to fall into the trap of depression and negative thinking. Perhaps the company was not generating good profits even before the business loss. Grateful individuals may view the loss as a sign from God to rethink their business strategy—perhaps by diversifying or redirecting their energy toward another venture. Thus, they can identify opportunities within the challenges they encounter. They are more likely to remain emotionally stable and discover solutions to those challenges.

A recent study by Shanyan Lei et al. from Zhejiang University School of Medicine in Hangzhou, China, examined how gratitude influences post-traumatic growth in patients who underwent coronary stent implantation. The study was published in January 2025 and revealed both direct and indirect positive effects. First, gratitude directly impacted recovery positively. Secondly, it had an indirect positive effect through the mediating influences of higher resilience and perceived social support.

Self-Esteem boosted

A consistent practice of gratitude reduces a person's tendency to make unfavourable comparisons and feel envious of those who have more. Instead of engaging in self-criticism or yearning for what they lack, individuals recognize and appreciate their achievements. This self-awareness boosts self-esteem and cultivates a more positive self-image.

Improved sleep quality

A bedtime routine that involves reflecting on what we are grateful for each day calms and relaxes the mind. We can achieve this through journaling or simply contemplating the positive experiences in our lives. Feeling content promotes sound and restful sleep.

The following section will examine how practising gratitude positively affects our physical health.

Physical Health Gains

Gratitude practice works its magic through a wholehearted acceptance of the present moment and an appreciation for our blessings. It remains to be seen how this affects the various systems in the body.

Improves Heart Health and Blood Pressure

It is widely recognized that our brains regulate the functions of our hearts. Therefore, anything that generates negative feelings in our minds has a cascading effect on our hearts and circulatory systems. When an individual's defensive neural circuits are triggered by fear, anger, resentment, jealousy, and similar emotions, the heart reacts accordingly due to the brain-heart connection. Blood pressure rises, and the heart rate increases, harming heart health. Practising gratitude activates prosocial neural circuits, resulting in a decrease in heart rate and a decline in blood pressure.

S. Kyeong et al. from Yonsei University in the Republic of Korea conducted a study to examine the effects of gratitude and resentment on the heart. The study group practised gratitude, while the resentment intervention group was the control group. The researchers employed functional connectivity to assess the modulatory effect of gratitude on brain-heart interactions. They discovered that the average heart rate was significantly lower during the gratitude intervention than during the resentment intervention, along with improved emotion regulation and motivation.

That is why individuals with heart problems recover more quickly when they maintain a consistent gratitude practice. Additionally, those with high blood pressure experience a decrease in their blood pressure levels.

Strengthens Immune System

If your body's immune system is strong, you can fight diseases and infections better. Regular gratitude practice reduces stress by lowering the production of stress hormones like cortisol. Persistently high cortisol levels can weaken the immune system. We have various immune cells whose activity improves when we are not stressed. Natural Killer cells, T Lymphocytes, B Lymphocytes, Macrophages, T Regulatory cells, and Dendritic cells neutralize and destroy harmful pathogens entering our body and dead cells. Additionally, natural killer cells target cancerous cells.

All these cells function best when a positive and relaxed mindset is cultivated through a consistent gratitude practice.

Reduces Inflammatory Processes

Gratitude reduces inflammation in the body, which can lead to various diseases over time. In 2021, researchers L. I. Haslett and colleagues at the University of California, Los Angeles, conducted a study investigating the neural mechanisms underlying the health benefits of gratitude in women.

This randomized controlled trial examined the effects of gratitude on inflammation. Prosocial circuits were activated, while threat-responsive circuits, influenced by the amygdala, were dampened. The amygdala is critical in triggering inflammation as part of the response to threats. Practising gratitude reduces cellular inflammatory responses, thereby promoting overall health.

Intensifies the Feeling of Well-being and reduces Muscle Tension.

Sometimes, we are surprised that a friend with severe arthritis still seems happy whenever we meet. These individuals are not pretending. The brain releases endorphins by focusing on the many blessings in life despite experiencing painful health problems.

Known as the "feel-good chemicals," these neurotransmitters enhance mood, reduce stress, alleviate pain, and improve well-being. Thus, a shift in attitude is very helpful in managing chronic pain conditions. Tight muscles, which stem from negative emotions, become relaxed, alleviating physical discomfort.

Optimizes Lung Function

Gratitude practices that incorporate conscious deep breathing and mindfulness facilitate lung expansion, thereby increasing the amount of oxygen delivered to the body. Elevated oxygen levels are beneficial for everyone.

In certain conditions, such as asthma and chronic obstructive pulmonary disease, the airways in the lungs can become constricted due to tightening the muscles lining the airways. Gratitude practices help relax and open the airways, providing benefits for these conditions.

Better Digestive System

Stress negatively impacts the digestive system. When individuals experience negative emotions such as resentment, anger, fear, jealousy, self-doubt, and depression, they may experience digestive issues.

Common problems include irritable bowel syndrome, acidity, and bloating. Practising gratitude helps reduce stress and promotes better digestion.

The advantages of a gratitude mindset span various aspects of life: it promotes longevity, increases energy levels, encourages the development of healthy habits, and slows the ageing process, enabling us to look many years younger than our chronological age.

Now, let us proceed to the next chapter, which explores how we can find something to be grateful for in our daily lives.

- **Gratitude Activates the Brain's Prosocial Circuitry** – Gratitude is a social emotion that engages the medial prefrontal cortex (MPFC), a brain region responsible for decision-making, generosity, and positive emotions. It enhances prosocial behaviours, such as cooperation and kindness, while reducing threat responses associated with the amygdala.

- **Gratitude Practices Strengthen Neural Pathways** – The brain has two opposing neural circuits: prosocial and defensive. While defensive circuits dominate for survival reasons, practising gratitude helps strengthen the prosocial pathways, resulting in long-term happiness, reduced stress, and increased resilience.

- **Neuroplasticity Enhances the Long-Term Effects of Gratitude** – The brain operates on a "use it or lose it" principle. Regular gratitude practice strengthens positive neural pathways while weakening negative, defensive circuits. Over time, this leads to greater resilience, emotional stability, and an increased ability to identify growth opportunities even in challenges.

- **Lower Incidence of Depression and Stress** – By shifting focus from what is lacking to what we have, gratitude promotes happiness and reduces stress levels. Practising gratitude helps individuals, especially those with chronic illnesses, feel more peaceful and accepting of their conditions, leading to a decrease in depression over time.

- **Boosts Self-Esteem** – Practicing gratitude regularly diminishes unfavourable comparisons, envy, and self-criticism. Instead, people begin to value their achievements, nurturing a more positive self-image.

- **Improves Heart Health and Lowers Blood Pressure**—Gratitude activates prosocial neural circuits, lowering heart rate and blood pressure. Studies confirm that those practising gratitude have better heart health and faster recovery from heart problems.

- **Reduces Inflammation and Strengthens the Immune System** – Studies show that gratitude dampens the brain's threat response circuits, reducing cellular inflammatory responses. Lower inflammation helps prevent chronic diseases and enhances the immune system.

- **Optimizes Lung Function** – Gratitude, when paired with mindful deep breathing, enhances lung function and oxygen delivery.

- **Aids Digestion** - It alleviates stress-related digestive problems such as bloating, acidity, and irritable bowel syndrome (IBS).

CHAPTER 3

GRATITUDE IN EVERYDAY LIFE

"Gratitude helps you to grow and expand; gratitude brings joy and laughter into your life and into the lives of all those around you."

– *Eileen Caddy*

We should not practice gratitude out of compulsion simply because we desire good things in life from that practice. Instead, we can strive to cultivate a grateful mindset that allows us to appreciate each moment, whether it brings joy or sorrow. In good times, we relish our blessings with thankfulness; in difficult times, we seek the silver lining and look for hidden opportunities within obstacles. Therefore, to cultivate a gratitude mindset, we aim to feel:

GRATITUDE IN THE SMALL THINGS AND HAPPENINGS

You woke up in the morning. It's time to be grateful for the gift of waking up and to recognize that you are one of the fortunate ones. Every morning, thousands of people around the world do not wake up; they die in their sleep.

Gratitude for Good Health

Compare yourself not with those who enjoy better health than you, but with those who lack the health blessings you possess.

A story about the ungrateful beggar.

A beggar sitting on the footpath complained and berated God for making him so poor.

"God, why are you so unkind?"

A passerby stopped and told him, "You are not poor; you are wealthy."

The beggar felt furious at this admonition and began to reproach him for mocking him.

At this, the passerby said to him, "I'm not mocking you. You can make a million dollars today."

"How?" the beggar asked, curious.

"Sell me your eyes, and I'll give you fifty thousand dollars."

"Are you mad? How will I get around anywhere if I sell you my eyes?"

"Why not? Millions of people around the world live without vision. You could sell me just one of your eyes for twenty-five thousand dollars if you want."

"No!"

"All right! We can consider other options. How about selling me your hands for a hundred thousand dollars?"

"You're out of your mind! How can I do anything without hands?"

"Why not? Thousands of people worldwide have lost their hands. For a fraction of the money you would get from selling your hands, you can acquire an artificial hand that is suitable for managing your life effectively."

"NOOO!"

The passerby sighed. "You're hard to please. All right then, how about just one of your hands for fifty thousand dollars?"

"No, not again!"

"Oh dear, no again! Well then, how about your legs for a hundred thousand dollars?"

"What's wrong with you? What would a hundred thousand dollars mean to me if I can't walk?"

"There you go again. You are deliberately being difficult. Haven't you seen people without legs? It is not uncommon to lose limbs in an accident. Millions of people cope very well. Moreover, there is plenty of assistance available these days. You will handle it just fine."

"Nooooo! I don't want to talk to you. I'm leaving this place."

"All right! Please don't get upset with me. I'm helping you make a lot of money quickly. If you're not comfortable with the solutions I've offered, let's think of other options. Now, let's explore what else you can sell. Tell me, can you breathe, eat, smell, taste, hear, and feel the touch of your loved ones?"

"Yes, of course, I have all these abilities. How does that concern you?"

"I am offering you ten thousand dollars for any of these skills. How does that sound for generosity?"

"What's wrong with you? You keep on asking me to sell my body parts and my abilities for money. I'm not going to listen to you."

"It's your mindset that is misaligned. God has bestowed great wealth upon you, yet you complain instead of utilizing what you possess. You constantly lament the material things you lack. Why would God grant you anything more if you are ungrateful for what you have and fail to use it well?"

" Ohhhh! Now I understand what you're saying. From now on, I will be grateful to God for these gifts and use them wisely to build a good life for myself and my family."

We can be grateful for our lives, including our capacity to *breathe* well. However, thousands of people experience such difficulty with breathing that they require continuous oxygen support to survive.

If our *hearts* function effectively and circulate oxygen-rich blood to all the cells in our bodies, we can choose to feel grateful. However, millions of individuals suffering from heart failure or rhythm disorders face challenges every day.

If our *brains* function efficiently, enabling us to discern, analyze, and make meaningful decisions based on our past experiences or the data from others, it presents an opportunity for gratitude. Millions of individuals with brain function issues encounter severe challenges. Alzheimer's disease, Parkinson's disease, dementia, major head injuries, strokes, and brain hemorrhages are just a few examples.

If we possess all *our limbs* and they are functioning well, we should be grateful. Millions of people have lost one or more limbs, or are unable to use their hands or legs due to nerve disorders.

If our body organs—heart, liver, lungs, pancreas, digestive system, kidneys, and endocrine system—are in good health, we should be grateful. Our health suffers badly when any of these organs go on strike or malfunction.

Appreciate the Beauty of Nature

We have become so accustomed to rushing through our lives, focusing on work, meetings, housework, shopping, and so on, that we fail to notice the splendor that nature presents to us. It is time to pause and appreciate the abundance and beauty of the natural world. If you believe in God, thank Him for this experience. If you don't believe in God, then the Universe, or any higher powers you acknowledge, deserve your gratitude. Indeed, we cannot claim to be the creators of this beauty.

When you wake up and look out your window, you may witness a beautiful sunrise. Take a moment to absorb the beauty of the early morning sun. You can also express gratitude to the sun for being there daily and providing life-giving energy to you and everything in the world. If the sun were absent, there would be no life anywhere. Whenever possible, please spend some time in the sun, feeling its warmth enveloping you.

You may travel to work in your vehicle or use public transportation. If you are in your car, it's difficult to appreciate the beauty of nature along the way because your focus is on the road and the traffic around you. First, try not to rush while traveling. Leave your home a few minutes early to savor your journey. If you notice something beautiful—perhaps a garden by the roadside filled with vibrant flowers, buzzing bees, fluttering butterflies, or singing birds—take a moment to stop. If time permits, you can enter the garden and sit on the grass. Enjoy the wonder of the delicate flowers, exquisitely crafted by nature. The magnificent butterflies and handsome bumblebees flitting between the flowers enhance the garden's allure. As you appreciate and give thanks for experiencing nature's charm, your mind relaxes, reducing any stress you may be feeling. This may help you find useful solutions to your current problem.

In addition to appreciating the beauty of nature we encounter every day, let's reflect on how we can enhance our appreciation for the experiences in our daily lives.

POWER OF MINDFUL APPRECIATION

Mindfulness enhances our sense of gratitude. Small, everyday occurrences that we often take for granted transform into Thanksgiving moments when we embrace them with appreciation, viewing them as gifts rather than entitlements.

Appreciation for clean drinking water and electricity

Clean water is something we often take for granted and, many times, waste unnecessarily. This brings to mind a TED Talk by Brother David Steindl-Rast about the importance of gratitude. He describes how he began to notice water after returning from a region in Africa where access to drinking water was difficult. Upon his return, he felt overwhelmed every time he turned on the tap and water flowed. He was filled with joy each time he clicked the light switch and the room was illuminated. However, over time, that happiness faded, and he began to take water and electricity for granted. To combat this, he developed a method to remind himself to be grateful for these essentials. He placed small stickers on the tap and light switch as reminders.

Brother David is a Benedictine monk, popularly known as the 'grandfather of gratitude'. Even he reminds himself to be grateful for everyday things. This means that, as we rush mindlessly through our daily grind, we must remind ourselves even more of the ordinary things to appreciate. As we continue our journey toward greater mindfulness and gratitude for life's offerings, it will transform our lives.

Gratitude for my home

When we see homeless people living in shelters or on the streets, we realize what a blessing our home is. I thank God for providing this roof over my head; it gives me security and comfort at all times.

Thankfulness for food

There are millions of people in the world who cannot afford even one meal each day, let alone two or three. Thank God I never have to go to bed hungry. I am grateful to have the freedom to eat whatever I want. When we consume our food with mindful appreciation, our absorption and digestion improve, leading to better health.

Gratitude for the comfortable bed, chairs and table for rest and work

Millions of people lack comfortable beds for sleeping. Thank you, God, for this cozy bed that gives me a good night's rest, allowing me to wake up refreshed in the morning for another wonderful day. And thank you, God, for the comfortable tables and chairs that allow me to work for long periods without feeling tired.

Gratitude for the cool, refreshing breeze produced by the fan and air conditioner.

When I compare myself to the millions of individuals who work in intense heat without the relief of a fan, I feel blessed. I am truly grateful for the appliances that provide a cool breeze during extremely hot weather. They help me feel refreshed and energized even after long hours of work.

Appreciation for the Piped Natural Gas used for Cooking

I am very grateful for the convenience of natural gas for cooking. I no longer have to light a wood fire each time, and I can cook whenever I want without being exposed to the smoke that comes with wood fires.

Gratitude for my vehicle.

I am so happy and thankful that my car conveniently takes me wherever I wish to go, so I don't waste time waiting for public transportation.

Thankful for my laptop and mobile phone.

I am so grateful that I live in this age of advanced technology. My smartphone instantly connects me to friends and family, wherever they may be in the world. With its help, I never feel alone or neglected. My laptop connects me to whatever information I search for with one click. Thank God for all the technology researchers who have made this possible.

Gratitude for My Income

Thank God for the regular income I receive each month. It allows me to provide my family and myself with a secure and comfortable life.

Our lives become richer when we savor the simple pleasures mindfully and do not take them for granted. We can enjoy hot coffee or tea on a chilly morning, feel the cosiness of our favorite blanket, appreciate refreshing water when we are thirsty, or admire the tall trees in the forest as sunlight filters through the leaves. When we pause to truly value everyday moments, life continually offers us more reasons to be thankful. There's something extraordinary about delighting in the coolness of water, the intense heat of fire, the warmth of the sun, clouds drifting in the sky, and the gentle caress of the breeze.

How can we turn ordinary moments into extraordinary ones when we interact with others? Let's explore.

TRANSFORMING ORDINARY MOMENTS

A story about a class of students and how they learned to appreciate one another

The primary school teacher wondered what she could do to prevent fights between groups of students in her class. Whenever she entered the class, she would find some quarrel going on. She was at her wits' end about how to make the students appreciate each other. One day, she thought of a plan.

She entered the class, broke up the ongoing brawl, and said, "Today I've thought of something very special for you people."

The students sat up straighter, fully attentive. "What, ma'am?" they asked.

"Have patience." She handed them each a blank sheet of paper. "Now, draw a line down the middle, dividing the paper into two parts."

The students looked at her with anticipation, wondering what she was planning next.

"Okay, think of your worst enemy in class and on the left side of the paper, write down all the bad qualities of this boy that you can think of."

All the students wrote busily without stopping, completely filling the left side. Once they finished writing, they looked at her with curiosity and wonder.

"Now, boys, jot down all the good qualities of your enemy on the right side of the paper."

Protests broke out - He doesn't have any good qualities, I can't think of a single one, he is bad through and through, nothing good about him.....

The teacher said firmly, "I don't want any excuses from you all. Nobody is inherently bad. Think deeply, and you will find something good. You have filled the left side of the paper completely with bad qualities. Find good qualities to fill at least half of the right side of the page."

This took the students significantly longer to write due to extended pauses between sentences. Ultimately, they finished.

"Now, please tear the paper along the line you drew in the middle."

Once they had done that, she continued, "Dispose of the left side of the paper containing the negative qualities in the dustbin and give the right side with the positive qualities to the boy you've written about."

The boys felt uneasy about giving this paper to their enemy, praising their good qualities, yet they complied with the directive. In the days that followed this exercise, their fights became less frequent, much to their teacher's relief. Perhaps when they felt the urge to start a fight with their enemy, they recalled the good qualities they had reluctantly written on the piece of paper. Many of them formed lifelong friendships.

So you see, when we think negatively about anyone, they seem all bad. When we start thinking in positive terms, there's a lot of good in them.

We interact with people or things at every moment of our lives, sending out an energy frequency. You may recall our discussion about the vibrational energies emitted by everything—both living and non-living. Negative emotions emit the lowest energy, with shame and guilt at the bottom. In contrast, gratitude, love, joy, and peace are at the higher end of the spectrum. Gratitude is closely linked with love and acceptance, both of which are high-frequency emotions.

The higher the energy frequency we emit, the more aligned we become with universal energies. Cultivating a mindset of gratitude naturally raises our frequency. As our connection to these universal energies deepens through the practice of gratitude, ordinary moments become transformed into magical experiences. How can one achieve this? Here's how:

Recognize Acts of Kindness

You are feeling a little under the weather. A friend stops by to see if you need anything from the market or help with housework. They are thinking of you during this time of need because they care about you.

You and your team worked diligently on the office project to meet the deadline. During the presentation of the completed project to the CEO, the team leader praised your contributions and acknowledged your hard Work.

A colleague holds the door to your office building open as you enter with your laptop, bag, and books.

All these small acts of kindness from people brighten our day. If we regularly acknowledge and appreciate them with love and gratitude, we can also help to brighten their day.

Appreciate our helpers

Many people work for us to keep our house and office organized, clean, and well-maintained. Without their help with essential tasks, we would struggle to accomplish our daily plans. Their support is crucial for us to continue our work. However, we often take them for granted and overlook their contributions instead of showing appreciation. Indeed, at times we find faults in their work. Why is that? Are we afraid that acknowledging their efforts will lead them to ask for a salary raise? This is usually not the case. Recognizing their sincere work with gratitude will make them happy, encouraging them to work with greater willingness and energy – a win-win situation for everyone.

Thanks to friends and family

An attitude of entitlement toward good wishes, gifts, and services from our loved ones can drive them away. Conversely, acknowledging their contributions to our lives makes a significant difference for both us and them, spreading happiness and goodwill all around. Their companionship and the harmonious atmosphere they create are invaluable.

Acknowledge neighbors' and strangers' kindness

Our immediate neighbors comprise our community. In unexpected emergencies, they often come to our aid, and vice versa. Therefore, it is essential to maintain loving relationships with them at all times. Expressing timely gratitude for their support is crucial to fostering long-term positive relationships.

A smile doesn't cost us anything. A kind smile directed at a helpful stranger brightens their day and makes them more inclined to be kind to others, creating a ripple effect of kindness and gratitude.

All of the above interactions, as well as similar ones, are minor incidents. As I have mentioned before, what resonates with others is not a specific incident but the frequency of your engagement. A higher frequency of acceptance and gratitude can transform your life and the lives of those around you.

So much for incorporating gratitude into our daily lives. Now, it is time to address the obstacles to practicing gratitude. Read on to recognize and surmount these barriers.

- **Gratitude Should Be Genuine, Not Forced** - Practicing gratitude should not be done out of obligation or to gain rewards but as a way to appreciate both good and bad moments in life.

- **Appreciate the Small Things in Life** - Waking up each morning is a blessing. Many people do not get this chance, so we should value each new day.

- **Be Thankful for Good Health** - Instead of comparing ourselves to those with better health, we should appreciate our ability to breathe, move, and function without struggle.

- **Nature Offers Endless Reasons for Gratitude** - We often rush through life without noticing the beauty of nature. Taking a moment to appreciate the sunrise, fresh air, or a blooming flower can bring peace and happiness.

- **Mindful Appreciation Transforms Life** - Gratitude deepens when we become mindful of the everyday conveniences we often take for granted, such as clean water, electricity, and a comfortable home.

- **Gratitude for Technology and Comfort** - Modern conveniences like fans, air conditioning, piped gas, vehicles, mobile phones, and laptops make life easier, and we should be grateful for these advancements.

- **Acknowledging Life's Simple Pleasures Enhances Joy** - Small joys, like a warm cup of tea, a cool breeze, or a cosy blanket, become meaningful when we truly appreciate them.

- **Recognizing Acts of Kindness Strengthens Relationships** - Expressing gratitude to friends, family, colleagues, and strangers for their small acts of kindness fosters stronger bonds and mutual goodwill.

- **Gratitude Elevates Energy and Vibration** - Positive emotions like love, joy, and gratitude emit high vibrational energy, attracting more positivity into life. What resonates with others is not a specific incident but the frequency of your engagement. A higher frequency of acceptance and gratitude can transform your life and the lives of those around you.

CHAPTER 4

BARRIERS TO GRATITUDE

"At times, our own light goes out and is rekindled by a spark from another person. Each of us has cause to think with deep gratitude of those who have lighted the flame within us."

– Albert Schweitzer

Life does not always follow a smooth trajectory. Ups and downs are essential. It is easy to feel thankful when everything is going well. However, one can lose the determination to remain grateful during difficult times. In these moments, individuals need to be even more vigilant in identifying things to appreciate to overcome challenges.

The most challenging time the world has faced in recent years was the **COVID-19 pandemic,** which began at the end of 2019 and reached all corners of the globe by the end of the first quarter of 2020. The whole world came to a standstill as LOCKDOWN came into force in every country. No one was allowed to travel from one country to another. In fact, travel within countries, even within cities, was severely restricted, with only the people manning essential services allowed to move under strict conditions.

Once a family member contracted Covid-19, they were swiftly moved to a hospital and placed in the Covid ward – an isolation area for patients suffering from the virus. No outsiders were allowed to meet them, not even their own family members.

With the lockdown in force, cities resembled ghost towns, with shops and malls shuttered and market areas, gardens, and parks deserted. The hospital OPDs, which used to overflow with patients during normal times, were now empty. Naturally, there was no question of visiting the hospital for minor issues. People avoided hospital visits even for major health concerns.

All services became available online, including doctor consultations, school and college studies, art and craft courses designed to keep people busy, and wellness courses, all transitioning from physical to online formats.

Many lives were lost during the various waves of Covid. Deaths were a lonely affair, with no one to offer support or commiserate with the grieving family. Similarly, joyful occasions like marriages were also solitary experiences, with no one to share in the family's happiness.

The pandemic lasted over two years, affecting many families' livelihoods and happiness. The world is still recovering from that impact. We can only thank God that we are alive and well today, able to contribute meaningfully to society.

Aside from the Covid-19 pandemic, life continues to present various challenges. Even someone who has cultivated a mindset of gratitude may struggle to find reasons for gratitude during extremely difficult situations.

For example, experiencing a substantial business loss that erases much of the market capital, enduring an unexpected road accident that leaves one immobilized with multiple fractures, dealing with a deceitful business partner who siphons off a significant amount of money, facing a major health crisis that drains most of one's savings, being evicted from home by family due to a dispute, or discovering that an elder in the family has been diagnosed with conditions like Parkinson's or Alzheimer's or other neurological illnesses with no hope for a cure- along with coping with painful, debilitating conditions such as severe arthritis—all these circumstances can make it challenging for a person to feel gratitude.

It is not suggested that one should feel gratitude for the challenging situation itself. However, there are ways to find *something* to be thankful for, even during these times. For example:

Discover Genuine Friends

It is often in the most difficult situations that we discover who our true friends and supporters are. When an individual experiences a significant business loss and needs the support of well-wishers to regain their footing, superficial friends will quietly drift away, leaving him alone. In this scenario, only true friends will remain to rally around him and help him stand back up.

Even if they cannot assist financially, small acts of kindness carry a lot of meaning. A comforting word, a gentle, caring touch, or simply knowing that this friend is there in support holds great value. Appreciating and being grateful for the support elevates one's energy levels and serves as a motivating factor to rise above the challenge.

> *"No one who achieves success does so without the help of others. The wise and confident acknowledge this help with gratitude."*
>
> *– Alfred North Whitehead*

Acknowledge Small Wins

In difficult times, it's easy to lose one's optimistic outlook and feel that only darkness lies ahead. When morning breaks and one doesn't feel like getting out of bed because there seems to be nothing to look forward to, simply mustering the energy to rise becomes a win, no matter how small. Completing the daily tasks of brushing teeth and having something for breakfast is another victory. If a morning walk has been an invigorating routine in the past, don't abandon it. Go for a walk; it can be brief if you don't feel up to a longer stroll. If the brain receives a positive message that circumstances aren't so dire, it will start to think likewise. This encourages thoughts of solutions rather than allowing you to remain trapped in problems.

Identify the stable features in your life.

If you still have the basic amenities in this challenging situation, you have much to be thankful for. It's fantastic that you have a roof over your head and a place to call home. If your daily food needs are met, that's something to appreciate. If your family supports you, that's something not everyone can boast about.

If you don't usually journal, start noting your blessings every day. Focusing on what you have instead of what you lack fosters a sense of security and stability. Concentrating on the aspects of your current situation that you can control empowers you. With this mindset, facing challenges and bouncing back from setbacks becomes easier.

Find opportunity in the challenge.

Often, we navigate life haphazardly. Perhaps we do not genuinely enjoy what we do, but since it provides the necessities for our lives, we seldom consider switching to something we prefer. A sudden, significant obstacle that arises in our routine could act as a wake-up call.

Opportunities come to those who actively seek them. The present challenge can also be a chance to learn—it may teach us resilience, patience, or self-discipline.

Regardless of the opportunity- whether it involves learning from our shortcomings or changing our life direction- embracing it with gratitude will make us stronger.

Sometimes, we find it difficult to overcome negativity and resentment towards those who have wronged us or towards the challenges we face in our lives. What is the way forward in such circumstances?

DEALING WITH NEGATIVITY AND RESENTMENT

Resentment toward someone for a perceived wrongdoing can wreak havoc on our lives. Not only that, but we often fall into a negative, complaining mindset, finding something to criticize or complain about in every situation, regardless of whether it affects us directly. A good example is when friends gather together; they may begin criticizing another friend who is absent that day, or they might lament the shortcomings of the local government, highlighting the many gaps in governance.

There are ways to overcome negativity so that the purpose of our lives remains on track, for example:

Acknowledge your Feelings of Negativity.

To overcome a negative mindset, it is crucial to first recognize that we nurture negative feelings. This is not to excuse negativity but to work towards overcoming it. Many individuals attempt to bury their feelings, believing that this equates to rising above negativity. However, this is a misconception. Suppressing resentment only makes it stronger, as we force it down into our subconscious mind. There, it continues to grow and thrive until, one day, the heightened resentment surges forth unexpectedly, much like water breaching a dam after a cloudburst.

Acknowledging our resentment without self-judgment allows us to experience our true feelings. We can then consciously choose not to dwell on that emotion and instead shift our focus to gratitude.

Recognize the Silver Lining

It is a well-known fact that every dark cloud has a silver lining. When facing challenges, instead of becoming discouraged by their weight, one should look for blessings, no matter how small they may be. If nothing else, the feeling of being wrongly accused of neglecting work will be alleviated by the knowledge that you have worked sincerely. Show kindness to yourself by appreciating your efforts. If, despite your efforts, only limited progress has been made, be grateful for that progress, however small.

Focus on Your Priorities

When life throws a double whammy at us, we encounter many individuals who simply give up under the weight of that misfortune. A shift in perspective is necessary to overcome a giving-up mindset. There are bound to be some things we can control and some things we can appreciate.

A story about priorities

Mark attended a business meeting with his clients. When the participants could not finish the agenda within the allotted time, Mark requested that they schedule another meeting for the following day to address the remaining agenda items.

The client asked, "Why not spend some more time now to finalize it?"

"I can't do that. I need to reach the nursing home by 4 pm to see my wife."

"What happened to her?"

"She has Alzheimer's disease, and I've had to keep her there for long-term care."

"Oh! Does she know who you are?"

Mark responded with, "No."

The client was confused. "Then why is it so important to be on time? Being an hour late won't make a difference."

Mark replied, "She doesn't recognize me as her husband, but I know she is my wife, and I love her. I will do everything in my power to keep her comfortable and happy. She knows that a kind person visits her every day at 4 pm, and she eagerly awaits this visitor. I am so grateful to God that even when she doesn't recognize me as her husband, I can lift her spirits and ensure her comfort. That is enough for me. Now, we can conclude this meeting, and I will contact you to schedule the next one."

When confronted with a misfortune like this, Mark was still able to find something he could control: ensuring his wife's happiness and comfort. For this, he was grateful to God.

List the Things You are Grateful For

Depression and resentment strengthen the threat-response neural circuits in our brains when we fixate on what is going wrong in our lives. To counter this amygdala hijack, we need to activate the prosocial neural circuits in our brains. Practicing gratitude is an effective way to achieve this.

I do not claim that negative emotions will disappear immediately when one begins practicing gratitude, but a shift in feelings can be experienced almost instantaneously, and over time, positive emotions will begin to take precedence.

A simple but powerful way to practice gratitude is to start a daily gratitude journal and list everything you are thankful for. This can include anything from a warm cup of coffee and the sunshine on your skin to having a supportive friend by your side.

Repeatedly, we meet individuals who compare themselves unfavorably to others. Is there anything that can be done about this? Let's investigate.

LETTING GO OF COMPARISON AND EMBRACING SELF-WORTH

Today's world has become a rat race driven by the insatiable expectations of a society that always demands more from us—

whether it's through social media platforms, the pressure to succeed, or the need to deliver even more.

Some individuals thrive on the adrenaline rush stemming from the ever-increasing societal expectations. For others, this environment can lead to excessive stress, resulting in a noticeable decline.

We may not match the stalwarts of the societal rat race, putting us at a disadvantage. It's easy to sink into the quicksand of comparison and struggle to stay afloat. Many aspiring media influencers and performers experience burnout as they attempt to meet public expectations.

How can we avoid feelings of low self-worth and excessive stress? By stopping comparing ourselves to others and looking inward to reflect on our own progress, we can feel happier and more confident.

To let go of negative comparisons:

Celebrate Your Unique Strengths

Every person in the world is unique, not only in appearance and personality but also in the lessons life has taught them, along with their talents, skills, and expertise in specific fields. Avoid viewing the achievements of others with envy. You possess many exceptional abilities and qualities that others may lack.

Take a moment to jot down what you excel at and what you have accomplished. If you do not value yourself, no one else will.

Compare with Yourself

Every person has their own path to tread at their own pace. Instead of feeling depressed or jealous when you see others who seem very successful, shift your focus to your own progress. How much have you advanced in the last few months? Have you learned from your past mistakes and become better? If you have improved even a little, that is something to celebrate.

Treat Yourself with Kindness

If a good friend of yours felt negatively about herself compared to others, what would you say to her? You would be patient and supportive, encouraging her to 'stop comparing yourself. '

No one is perfect; everyone makes mistakes. If you have made mistakes, accept them and learn from them to avoid repeating them in the future. That is what life is all about.

Define success by your own standards.

Living by your own values instead of others' expectations creates magic. Your definition of success may vary greatly from society's. When you live on your own terms and value what you have achieved, peace and fulfillment are yours.

As we move into the next chapter, let's explore how gratitude can enhance our relationships.

- **Gratitude in Hard Times** – It's easy to be grateful when life is smooth, but during difficult times, making an effort to find things to appreciate helps overcome challenges.

- **Lessons from the COVID-19 Pandemic**—The pandemic disrupted lives globally, isolating people, affecting livelihoods, and reshaping how we function, yet we should be grateful for surviving it.

- **Discovering Genuine Friends** – Hardships reveal who our true supporters are, as superficial friends disappear while true ones stand by us, offering emotional or practical support.

- **Acknowledging Small Wins** – Even in tough times, small accomplishments like getting out of bed, eating, or going for a short walk contribute to resilience and a positive mindset.

- **Recognizing Stability Amidst Struggles** – If basic needs like shelter, food, and family support are met, that is something to appreciate, fostering security and stability.

- **Finding Opportunity in Challenges**—Difficulties often force people to reflect, which can lead to discovering new opportunities, resilience, patience, or even a more fulfilling path.

- **Overcoming Negativity and Resentment**: Acknowledge negative emotions without suppressing them. Every dark cloud has a silver lining. Appreciate blessings, no matter how small. This helps shift focus toward gratitude, preventing bitterness from taking over.

- **Letting Go of Comparison** – Constantly comparing oneself to others leads to stress and low self-worth, while focusing on personal growth and unique strengths fosters confidence.

- **Defining Success on Your Own Terms** – Society's expectations may be overwhelming, but true fulfillment comes from aligning with one's own values and standards of success.

- **The Power of Gratitude Practices** – Keeping a gratitude journal, recognizing personal progress, and appreciating small joys can rewire the brain to focus on positivity and well-being.

Chapter 5

Gratitude And Relationships

"Feeling gratitude and not expressing it is like wrapping a present and not giving it."

– William Arthur Ward

We can categorize Relationships into two types: communal relationships and exchange relationships. Intimate connections among family members, romantic partners, and close friends fall into the communal relationship category. Individuals share deep interpersonal bonds within the community, fostering a sense of shared responsibility through support and care for one another. There are no expectations of quid pro quo or specific returns. First, let's examine how gratitude contributes to maintaining healthy family dynamics.

GRATITUDE IN FAMILY DYNAMICS

Connections with family are among the most significant relationships in our lives. Although we love our family dearly, taking them for granted is common. Misunderstandings or differences among family members may arise for various reasons. The stress and hurt feelings can disrupt the family's joyful togetherness. Consciously developing a gratitude practice fosters a supportive atmosphere, allowing interpersonal bonds to grow stronger and more loving.

Expressing gratitude isn't merely a formal 'thank you. 'Genuine appreciation for their efforts or gifts embodies the true essence of gratitude.

Many argue about gratitude to one's family for the services and benefits we often take for granted. Here, the long-term negative impact of a sense of entitlement becomes clear. Gratitude plays an essential role in continuing to nurture deeper and warmer relationships.

Create gratitude rituals as a family activity.

A family's anecdote about their gratitude practice

A family I know has created an innovative way to ensure that each member appreciates the good things happening in their lives. Their parents keep a piggy bank in a visible spot in the house. I was with them once when their son came home from school after winning a race at the annual sports day. He and the entire family were pleased. Their parents promised to celebrate his victory with an outing in the evening. Then, he approached the piggy bank and deposited some money into it.

I asked with curiosity, "Why is he doing that?"

His mother answered, " He has placed some of his pocket money in the piggy bank. Our family has a gratitude ritual. When someone receives something they appreciate, they drop some money into the piggy bank. Once it is full, we open it and take out the money. Then, we all go out together to give it to someone in need or donate it to an organization that supports social welfare. When we see the happiness of the person receiving the donation, our faces also light up with joy. This way, the children are cultivating the habits of gratitude and charity."

I was impressed: "What an ingenious idea!"

Another gratitude ritual can take place during mealtimes. A family should share at least one meal each day. Smartphones, laptops, books, and newspapers should be kept away from the dining table. Family members can share their experiences, especially the positive moments they encounter throughout the day. This way, the entire family expresses gratitude for the good experiences, while the family's support and advice soften any unpleasant events of the day.

Practice Active Listening and appreciating

When a family member comes to share something weighing on their mind—whether it's good news, a request for advice, or a plea for a purchase—we often become preoccupied with our priorities.

If we listen with half-hearted attention, we often miss the core issue. Our greatest gift to our family is our undivided attention when they need it. We should be grateful that they wish to share something significant to them. Therefore, we can express our gratitude by listening attentively and responding kindly when necessary.

A family member with a passion or exceptional talent needs nurturing. Recognizing and valuing each family member's unique abilities and strengths boosts their self-esteem and contributes to their success in life.

Acknowledge Contributions and Efforts

Recognizing their contributions to the family unit will enhance their self-esteem and motivate them to contribute more. This may involve willingly offering assistance when needed, making genuine efforts regardless of the outcome, using creativity and imagination to develop something new, or a spouse providing support even at the expense of their obligations. Whatever is done with good intentions deserves to be acknowledged with love. This approach will further strengthen family bonds.

A daughter's contribution to the family

Sarah was an outstanding student who consistently earned A+ grades in her schoolwork. Now, in her senior year, she loves math and excels at solving any math problem.

Suddenly, her father experienced a significant loss in his business due to a stock market crash. He had borrowed money and heavily invested in stocks, planning to sell them when prices increased. His market capital was completely wiped out. Thankfully, their home had not been mortgaged, so it remained theirs. However, over time, managing day-to-day expenses became challenging, accompanied by reminders from creditors for repayment. When creditors learned of the stock market crash, they immediately sought to recover their money.

Sarah was the oldest child in the family. She decided to do something for them. Utilizing social media, she offered her services as a private mathematics tutor for primary school students struggling with the subject. While keeping up with her schoolwork, she began providing weekly home tuition to give personalized attention to the areas where each child needed assistance. Before long, she gained popularity and was in high demand.

Her father appreciated her much-needed contribution to the family kitty. However, he discouraged her from accepting any more tuitions that would have taken away from the time she required for her studies.

With strong self-esteem and motivation, Sarah excelled in her final year at school and was admitted to an engineering institution of her choice for further study.

Recall Happy Family Memories

Gathering and reminiscing about the joyful moments the family shares is valuable. In today's digital age, photographs are stored digitally, while older photos remain in albums. As we flip through old pictures, memories come alive. Reflecting on anecdotes and experiences from the past nurtures a sense of togetherness within the family.

Next, we will explore how gratitude can strengthen romantic relationships.

DEEPER ROMANTIC RELATIONSHIPS THROUGH APPRECIATION.

If gratitude and appreciation are ingrained in a partnership, they establish a strong foundation of love and trust. Numerous studies have been conducted on this topic over the years. One study by S. B. Algoe et al. in 2010 was titled, 'It's the Little Things: Everyday Gratitude as a Booster Shot for Romantic Relationships. '

The researchers explored gratitude and indebtedness as responses to costly, intentional benefits provided by others. They found that while gratitude strengthened the relationship, feelings of debt did not. A recipient feels indebted when they perceive an expectation to repay the benefit given by the giver.

The study concluded that even in close, intimate relationships, gratitude transforms ordinary moments into opportunities for growth.

A tale of a couple's secret to happiness

Albert and Heather's 50th wedding anniversary was approaching. Their three children gathered at their house to plan a celebration. Heather did not want a large party; she preferred a small get-together with close friends and family. However, her husband and children overruled her and insisted on a big celebration.

She told Albert, "Many of our friends are alone now, losing their partners either through death or divorce. They might not feel good at the party. Close friends and family are a different matter."

Some family members disagreed so the children organized the party.

At the party, one of the guests remarked, "You folks have spent 50 years together. One might have thought you would have grown bored with each other long ago. Yet, look at you—you seem as happy as you were on your wedding day. How do you manage it?"

Heather and Albert exchanged glances and smiled. Heather said, " We know an amazing secret to happiness. Would you like to hear about it?"

All the guests had gathered around them by that time. A chorus arose, exclaiming, "Yes, please!"

"Will you tell them about it, or should I?" Heather asked her husband.

"You can go ahead," Albert replied.

"Okay, friends, it's not that we never fight or disagree. Like any normal couple, we have our share of disagreements. However, there's one small difference compared to those who become distant due to growing differences."

Another chorus asks, "What's the difference?"

Heather said, "In the early years of our marriage, we often quarrelled and dwelled on each other's shortcomings. Then we realized how we were wasting our happiness. We made a pact and solemnly promised to uphold it. The pact? Well, it was this—every night, we shared one thing we were grateful for about each other."

A friend asked, "Is that all?"

Heather responded, "Yes! Try it out. It's a powerful recipe for happiness. After this pact, even when we quarrelled, our fights didn't spill over into the next day because, at night, we had to find something to be grateful for in each other. The anger dissipated since you can't simultaneously hold gratitude and anger towards a person."

To cultivate gratitude in a relationship, we can consciously express appreciation and thankfulness for the small positive moments in our daily lives:

Express Gratitude for the Little Things

It's easy to take one another for granted in a long-term partnership. Small, caring gestures work wonders to draw you closer. Your spouse lovingly hands you a cup of hot coffee in the morning. Before you leave for work, the housework is quickly completed, with both of you contributing. At times, the wife may include a loving note with the tiffin for the mid-morning coffee break at the office. How we respond to such small, thoughtful gestures determines how much deeper the relationship can grow. Gratitude can be expressed by preparing a favourite dish as a thank you, bringing home some of her favourite flowers, and showing appreciation for the coffee with a smile and a kiss. All these small acts of gratitude enhance the intimacy and depth of the relationship.

Replace Complaints with Appreciation

It is neither necessary nor desirable for us to like everything about our spouse. The well-known saying that 'opposites attract' is proven accurate repeatedly. We are drawn to what we lack. For example, an introverted, quiet man may be attracted to an extroverted, vivacious woman, and vice versa. Years after marriage, the qualities that once attracted him may become irritating, leading him to complain about them. There may be other qualities about the partner that were overlooked at the beginning of the relationship but now feel unbearable.

When you focus on the qualities of your partner you love instead of those you dislike, life becomes more positive and effortless. Recall a time when you faced a challenge, and your partner stepped in to effortlessly resolve the issue. Frequently reminding yourself of their good qualities, kindness, and support will further deepen your connection.

Anticipate their Desires and Needs.

In today's work-from-home culture, there are times when one partner tries to concentrate on an office project but struggles because the children frequently enter the room and disturb them. The children are simply being themselves, not intentionally intrusive. The other partner may take the children out for a few hours to create an uninterrupted period for work.

One partner is unwell and needs quiet time to rest and regain energy. However, with small, energetic children in the house, achieving such quiet time is not easy. Once again, a supportive partner can take the children on an extended outing, such as to the local museum, zoo, or a children's movie, allowing for the necessary quiet rest time.

One partner completed a challenging project in record time, and for this achievement, they received a long-overdue promotion. The other partner's surprise celebration party will further boost their spirits and sustain their motivation.

Focus on Conflict Resolution, not Escalation

Whenever more than one person is present, disagreements and conflicts are inevitable. If there are never any disagreements in a partnership, one partner may be suppressing their feelings, staying quiet to maintain peace or out of fear of voicing their opinions.

First, we must realize that, as unique individuals, our thoughts cannot be identical. No one is perfect, and no one is right all the time. During conflicts, focus on the other person's positive qualities. If we concentrate on flaws, it can open a Pandora's box.

Recognizing the positive helps us resolve conflicts more quickly. My mentor has a rule: if there's a disagreement with her spouse, she ensures it is addressed and resolved before bed. That makes sense. At night, whatever occupies our conscious mind descends into the subconscious. Once there, it can build up quietly until it erupts like a volcano. Prompt resolution prevents it from simmering within us. Nowadays, we hear many stories about couples visiting marriage counsellors or going through a divorce.

It may have started with a trivial disagreement that escalated into a crisis. So, yes, that's sound advice.

Do the same principles apply in friendships, or is there a difference? Let us see.

GRATITUDE IN FRIENDSHIP

There are several subtypes of friendship: friendships cultivated for material gain, friendships formed for mutual benefit, friendships among business partners, and the most essential type—friendships where there is a heartfelt connection. Friendships can only thrive when we genuinely engage with friends and acquaintances and with inherent kindness.

There are many ways to express gratitude to friends:

Give Thoughtful Compliments

Often, we only appreciate our friends' positive qualities in our minds without expressing these thoughts openly. You must communicate with your friends and others about what you value in them.

These qualities may include their ability to recover from challenging financial or emotional situations, sense of humour, or kindness toward people and animals. A sincere compliment can uplift their spirits, enhance their self-worth, and strengthen your relationship with them.

Express gratitude frequently, but make sure it is genuine.

When your friend offers support, their time, or something valuable, acknowledge it with gratitude. Not everyone has the time or willingness to be there for you during tough times.

When you are going through a challenging period and a friend unexpectedly brings you a homemade meal, a thoughtful card, or a small gift, it shows they are thinking of you. A heartfelt 'Thank you' goes a long way in strengthening and maintaining friendships.

Be with them when they need you

Genuine gratitude involves more than just receiving support. Be there for others during their tough times. Offering assistance or simply being present with them brings emotional strength.

A narrative on timely assistance

The exam was in three days, and Amos felt disheartened. Calculus was his bête noire. He struggled to understand the concepts and master the subject, feeling like giving up. He confided in his friend Chinmay about his feelings.

"I'll skip the exam this time and prepare more effectively for the next one," Amos told Chinmay.

"You still have three days before the exam. Let's do this: I will spend time with you today and tomorrow to help you grasp the subject better. If you feel confident, take the exam; otherwise, there's always next time," Chinmay said encouragingly.

Amos said gladly, "Okay, let's do it."

For the next two days, Chinmay stayed with Amos and patiently explained the basics of the subject until Amos grasped it. Afterwards, he had Amos practice various problems for several hours, continuing late into the night.

When the day of the examination arrived, Amos felt confident and well-prepared. He tackled the exam with ease and left the exam hall smiling. Later that day, he visited Chinmay's house with a box of marshmallows, knowing how much Chinmay loved them.

When Amos handed the box to Chinmay, he exclaimed, "Oooooh! Lovely! But why?"

"Just to acknowledge your unwavering support and help. I have always valued your friendship and value it even more now," Amos responded.

Celebrate Their Successes

When your friend achieves success, be sure to celebrate their accomplishments. It doesn't matter whether the milestone reached or the reason for the celebration is big or small. Perhaps you are simply celebrating her birthday. There could also be a more significant reason to celebrate—a promotion, a new job opportunity, or a personal health goal like losing 5 kg.

The 'Just like that' Check-in

It is wonderful when someone reaches out and checks in without apparent reason. This sentiment is especially meaningful for those who are living and managing everything independently.

A 'Just stopped by to say hello' story

Neha stirred restlessly in her sleep. Sleep had evaded her for hours that night, and when she finally drifted off, it was a fitful rest. When morning came, she didn't feel refreshed. It was time to rise, so she slowly got out of bed and began her morning routine.

Usually, she was cheerful and engaged with one thing or another, but today was different. Occasionally, she experienced these unexpected days when a heavy mood settled over her.

Neha lived alone after retiring from her job at an accounting firm. Her husband had passed away a few years earlier, and her children resided in other cities with their families. They visited her almost every year, filling the house with laughter and the playful antics of her grandchildren. The phone rang, pulling her out of her reverie. Her friend Pari was calling. She was nearby and asked if she could drop by for a few minutes. Neha felt very happy and replied, "Do come." When Pari arrived shortly afterwards, Neha's face lit up with joy at the sight of her friend. They settled onto the sofa and chatted while she turned on the gas stove to heat water for coffee.

Neha's mood brightened as they reminisced about their shared laughter and joyful moments.

She told her friend, "You are a godsend. I was feeling down today for no reason, and you came and lifted me out of it."

Pari replied, "That's what friends are for. I'm glad I came today."

Nostalgia

When you sit together, you often recall memories. Reminiscing about shared adventures and experiences is an excellent way to appreciate the time spent together. Cherishing old memories strengthens your bond and helps you realize how much your friends have enriched your life.

Does gratitude contribute to enhancing your workplace?

Let us move on to the next chapter, which discusses the workplace.

- **Two Types of Relationships** – We can categorize relationships as communal (family, close friends, romantic partners) and exchange-based (transactional relationships). Gratitude plays a vital role in strengthening communal bonds.

- **Gratitude in Family Dynamics** – Expressing genuine appreciation for family members fosters stronger bonds, reducing misunderstandings and entitlement.

- **Creating Gratitude Rituals** – Families can implement daily gratitude practices, such as sharing positive experiences during meals to strengthen connections.

- **Active Listening and Appreciation**—Giving undivided attention to family members when they share thoughts or emotions reinforces love and respect.

- **Acknowledging Efforts and Contributions** – Recognizing and valuing family members' contributions enhances their self-esteem and motivation.

- **Gratitude in Romantic Relationships** – Small gestures of appreciation, such as expressing thanks for everyday acts, can significantly deepen love and trust.

- **Focusing on Strengths, Not Flaws** – Replacing complaints with appreciation strengthens relationships by focusing on the positive aspects of a partner rather than their shortcomings.

- **Gratitude in Friendships** – Sincere compliments, celebrating successes, and checking in 'just like that' will deepen friendships by showing thoughtfulness and care.

- **Nostalgia Strengthens Bonds** – Revisiting shared memories with friends and family fosters appreciation for the time spent together, reinforcing meaningful relationships.

CHAPTER 6

GRATITUDE IN THE WORKPLACE

"He who blames others has a long way to go on his journey. He who blames himself is halfway there. He who blames no one has arrived"

- Lao Tse

Most people spend over half of their waking hours at work. When CEOs and top managers regularly express appreciation for their subordinates, this prosocial behaviour trickles down, boosting employee motivation.

Some studies have examined the impact of gratitude on employee behaviour. A survey by A.M. Grant and F. Gino (2010) explored how appreciation influences employees. They found that employees who received genuine gratitude from their managers were more productive and willing to assist their colleagues.

In contrast, the impact of ingratitude on employees has been extensively researched by

Christina Maslach. Maslach and her colleagues discovered that employees who feel unappreciated by their employers experience higher rates of burnout, decreased motivation, and a greater likelihood of resigning. Their 2009 article on burnout in Career Development International clarified these effects.

Organizations that promote gratitude and appreciation in the workplace create a robust professional environment. Let's examine how this impacts workplace culture.

INFLUENCE OF GRATITUDE ON WORKPLACE CULTURE

Boosts Employee Morale

Appreciation nurtures an employee's sense of belonging. When individuals feel valued, their morale improves, leading to greater enthusiasm and motivation in their work. They are more likely to put in extra effort to help the organization meet its commitments, which benefits the entire organization.

Reduces Burnout and Stress

When a manager effectively responds to an employee's needs and limitations while delegating work accordingly, it creates a healthy work environment and reduces stress. Occasionally, an employee may require encouragement to put in extra effort to complete a project on time. However, managing stress becomes simpler as the employee recognizes that this increased effort will not be needed indefinitely. Proper mental conditioning can help combat exhaustion and extreme stress effectively.

A narrative about supportive coworkers

Abhinav worked at a software consultancy firm. His team was assigned a project to develop software tailored to specific requirements within a tight timeline. All team members focused on different aspects of the software, continuously discussing and consulting with one another about the pros and cons of the designs and modifications they were creating.

One morning, as work was in full swing, Abhinav received a call from his wife. She was crying and barely able to speak. He learned that their son was seriously injured in a bike accident. She told him she was leaving for the hospital where their son had been taken and implored him to come as soon as possible.

Abhinav was stunned. He informed his colleagues about the accident, and they accompanied him to the manager's office, where he notified the manager and requested leave for the day. At the hospital, he and his wife met with the doctor, who explained the extent of the injuries: vital internal organs were affected, and multiple fractures were present. Thankfully, there were no head injuries since his helmet had protected his head. However, the other injuries were severe, and he would spend many days in the hospital. He would also require blood transfusions due to a considerable amount of internal bleeding. Abhinav called his best friend at the office to explain the situation.

Five of his colleagues and his friend arrived at the hospital within half an hour. They had come to donate blood for Abhinav's son. After donating blood, they assured Abhinav that they would speak with the management regarding his emergency. They would also take over his share of the project work and put in extra hours to complete it on time. The top management responded supportively, allowing Abhinav to care for his son easily.

Once his son recovered, he returned and worked extra hard to compensate for lost time. He then sent personal emails to top management and all his office colleagues expressing his gratitude for their support in his hour of need. The recipients appreciated these letters, which enriched their relationships.

Reduces Employee Turnover

A workplace that promotes a culture of gratitude improves employee retention. Everyone wants to remain in an organization where their contributions are acknowledged and appreciated. When employees feel they are an essential part of the organization, a positive emotional connection is formed, and they are more inclined to remain.

Enhances Team Relationships

A culture of gratitude fostered by leadership benefits everyone by promoting mutual respect and trust among employees rather than spreading mistrust and unhealthy competition. When colleagues value and appreciate each other's contributions, conflicts are minimized, which increases the likelihood of collaboration.

Office politics is often associated with cutthroat competition, as each employee tries to win favour with the boss and displace those selected for promotions. To achieve this, they may resort to either fair or unfair methods. This dynamic is aptly termed the rat race. The tactics of the rat race fail when the boss is unresponsive to or disapproves of unfair methods. Thus, anyone who has previously employed such tactics tends to align better and improve as they embrace gratitude instead of ingratitude.

Increases Productivity And Performance

When embedded in an organization's culture, gratitude leads to high employee motivation. In a knowledge-intensive company, where value relies on its workforce's intellectual capital and specialized knowledge, appreciation inspires employees to enhance client experiences through research-based insights and innovations.

In a factory or product-based company, employees respond to appreciation by increasing productivity and innovating to create higher-quality, cost-effective products. As a result, the organization's reputation improves in the eyes of potential clients.

Improves an Organization's Reputation

Organizations that promote a culture of gratitude attract top talent, and their reputations extend far and wide. Every company aims to cultivate a reputation for recognizing and valuing genuine work. Both clients and employees are drawn to engage with a gratitude-oriented company that is supportive and rewarding for everyone.

Now, let us examine the desired leadership qualities in this organization in the next section.

GRATITUDE IN LEADERSHIP

The practices established by an organization's top leadership shape the culture of subordinates. When leaders criticize and highlight faults in employees' actions, morale declines. Stress and burnout become prevalent, and employee turnover skyrockets.

Conversely, morale increases when the top leader recognizes and commends the employees' hard work, leading to a much higher retention rate.

Lead by Example

Leaders who publicly express appreciation for the high-quality work performed by employees set an example for the organization. This impacts how the managers beneath them interact with their subordinates. It may involve simple gestures, such as recognizing an employee's contribution in a meeting, personally calling them, or writing a handwritten note to commend their efforts.

Organize Special Recognition Events

Some companies arrange special programs to create opportunities for appreciation. For example, a valued employee might be surprised during a personal milestone (such as a birthday, 25th wedding anniversary, or the birth of a child) with a celebration planned by top leaders and organized by the rest of the staff.

Special gratitude programs can be established, like an 'Employee of the Month' award.

Provide Constructive Feedback

Appreciation combined with constructive feedback keeps employees motivated. If an employee submits a project report that falls short, criticizing them and focusing solely on their faults will cause morale to plummet. Instead, if the areas needing improvement are addressed kindly, along with acknowledging their strengths, it will create the necessary balance and keep them motivated.

Provide Concrete Rewards

Expressing appreciation to an employee during a meeting or personal call can raise the company's motivation level. However, employee motivation reaches new heights when paired with rewards such as bonuses or tangible tokens of appreciation. Employees feel genuinely valued by the organization.

Promote Open Communication

In a culture of gratitude, employees feel comfortable sharing their feedback, new product design ideas, and recent advancements in the field that they believe management should know about.

As communication channels remain open, subordinates can contact their superiors about any concerns. Therefore, communication and collaboration serve as practical tools within the company.

Now, let's explore an essential aspect of gratitude practice: how can we implement it?

Proceed to the next chapter.

- **Boosts Employee Motivation** – Employees who receive genuine appreciation from managers tend to be more productive and helpful toward colleagues.

- **Reduces Burnout and Stress** – Employees who feel unappreciated experience higher burnout rates, while gratitude from leadership fosters a healthier work environment.

- **Lower Employee Turnover**—Organizations that prioritize gratitude improve retention, as employees feel valued and form stronger emotional connections with the company.

- **Enhances Team Relationships** – A culture of gratitude promotes mutual respect, reduces conflicts, and minimizes office politics by discouraging unfair competition.

- **Improves Company Reputation** – Organizations known for valuing employees attract top talent and earn respect from clients and stakeholders.

- **Leaders Set the Tone** – When leaders express appreciation openly, it influences the entire organization, leading to a more positive workplace culture.

- **Constructive Feedback is Key** – Special programs like "Employee of the Month" and milestone celebrations help reinforce a culture of appreciation. Balancing appreciation with constructive criticism ensures employees remain motivated while improving their performance.

- **Encourages Open Communication** – A gratitude-driven workplace promotes transparency, making employees feel comfortable sharing ideas and concerns with management.

CHAPTER 7

THE PRACTICE OF GRATITUDE

"As we express our gratitude, we must never forget that the highest appreciation is not to utter words, but to live by them."

– John F. Kennedy

As I mentioned earlier in the book, gratitude is not a natural emotion for most people. Scientific studies have shown that the default setting of neural circuits in our brains is not happiness but defensive or threat-responsive circuits. These defensive circuits, mediated by the amygdala, are more prominent because they ensure our safety, both physically and psychologically.

We need to strengthen the gratitude-serving networks. Establishing a gratitude practice could result in joy and contentment. Consistent practice will lead to positive changes, making the prosocial neural circuits more dominant so that we remain positive even when we do not always engage in these practices.

Now, why is it essential to maintain a positive outlook? Anxiety-inducing or fear-provoking events frequently arise in our lives. When the amygdala takes control with the defensive circuits fully engaged, we may find it challenging to think and respond constructively. However, through a consistent gratitude practice, a shift in emotional pathways occurs, allowing us to raise our motivation to find viable solutions and take action when faced with a challenging situation.

Spiritual teachers, philosophers, scientists, and others who have explored and practised gratitude techniques have found many effective.

We can gain insights from these and tailor our practice to best suit us. So, let's begin:

MORNING GRATITUDE PRACTICE

When we wake up, the first and most important thing is to thank God, the Universe, or whoever we look up to for being alive. We must know that every day, thousands of people worldwide do not wake up.

Thank you, Universe, for the gift of another beautiful day.

We don't need to set aside a specific time for gratitude. As we go through our daily routines, we can appreciate everything that draws our attention. Expressing gratitude for each positive occurrence or item helps eliminate any tendency for negativity to creep in. When our mornings are filled with gratitude, we can remain positive throughout the day.

Comparisons should only be made with those who lack the blessings we enjoy.

We are blessed that:

- We were able to sleep comfortably in our bed.

- We have a roof over our heads that offers security and shields us from the elements.

- We have enough clean clothes to wear every day.

- We have food on the table, ensuring we never go to bed hungry.

- We have clean drinking water available freely.

- The bathroom is inside our house, so we don't have to go far outside.

- Piped gas is available for cooking, so we don't have to light a wood or coal fire whenever we want to cook anything.

- Electrical appliances that assist us are indeed a blessing. The light bulb, refrigerator, oven, heater, geyser for a hot bath, fan, and air conditioner all make our lives so much easier that any day they malfunction or an electricity outage occurs, perhaps due to overload, we find life unbearable. Please think of the times when they were not invented or available.

- Advancements in information technology allow us to access any information we seek with just a click, without having to travel long distances.

- Advancements in satellite communication allow us to connect with loved ones and others from any corner of the globe.

Everything we see or feel that has made our lives easier deserves our heartfelt gratitude.

GRATITUDE REMINDERS

Often, we decide to practice gratitude but are inconsistent with it. This inconsistency may arise because we forget or are unaware of its benefits.

We often take it for granted once we become accustomed to having something. It is only when it is absent that we recognize its actual value.

In a TED talk, Brother David Steindl-Rast shared his experience in a region of Africa where access to drinking water and electricity was limited. Upon his return, he felt grateful for having clean water when he turned on the tap and for the light that appeared when he flipped the switch. However, after a while, the novelty faded. To remind himself to be grateful, he placed stickers on the tap, and the light switch to remind him to appreciate these conveniences every time he used them.

Br. David Steindl-Rast refers to these reminders as 'STOP SIGNS.' We can create our stop signs using our imagination. They might be stickers on items, as he demonstrated, or something you feel comfortable with.

In his book *Thanks,* Robert A. Emmons recommends various methods for reminding oneself to be grateful. Some individuals prefer visual cues, such as post-it notes, placed in frequently seen areas like doors, refrigerators, mirrors, oven doors, washing machine tops, and other noticeable spots. These notes may list blessings or simply prompt appreciation for specific things. Other people set alarms at different times throughout the day. When the alarm rings, it signals them to pause and reflect on their blessings.

Emmons regards other people as valuable reminders. He suggests spending more time with positive, grateful individuals and less time with ungrateful individuals who complain about what they lack or criticize others' behaviour. Another option is to have an accountability partner who can periodically remind us to express gratitude. This support is especially crucial during challenging times when one needs encouragement to shift from counting complaints to counting blessings.

GRATITUDE JOURNALING

Journaling is one of the best ways to practice gratitude. You might think that writing is more like a tedious chore and that it should be enough to reflect on the blessings we enjoy. However, journaling takes us much deeper. Recording what we feel grateful for establishes a stronger connection to our inner selves. Both our subconscious and superconscious become engaged in the feeling of thankfulness. The goodness we write about is magnified, bringing happiness into our lives. One can set a specific time for journaling to incorporate it into the day's routine. Any convenient time works well – whether in the morning or before bed.

When you start journaling, begin by writing down all the things, events, and people in your life for which you feel thankful in the present moment. As you write, take the time to deeply feel your heart's gratitude. Don't just list what you appreciate, like my home, parents, running water, etc. Write complete sentences and elaborate on why you are grateful; for example, I am genuinely thankful for my beautiful home, which provides security and shelters me from the elements at all times.

When you begin writing, you may find that only a few things come to mind for which to be thankful. However, as you persist, your list will grow longer. You will recall more and more things to appreciate.

Once you finish your current list of things you're grateful for, take a moment to reflect on your future aspirations. Visualize having attained what you desire and revel in the joy of that item or experience. Write about receiving it and expressing gratitude for the acquisition as if it is happening in the present tense.

Our subconscious listens to what we tell ourselves and fulfils it. If you say, 'I want this to happen,' the wanting will continue in your life. If you say, 'I will get this in the future,' it will always stay in the future. To obtain something, you need to act as if you have already received it and thank the universe for it. The key is that you must genuinely believe you possess it.

If you know deep down that it is not there yet and still express gratitude for receiving it, it cannot happen. Faith is essential here. Have faith that the universe has granted you your desires, and give thanks accordingly; it will come to pass.

REFLECT ON YOUR LIFE

Life is not always a smooth journey; it resembles a roller-coaster ride filled with joyful moments interspersed with challenging times that require grit and determination. You have survived these harsh periods and emerged as a winner. Well, if not a winner, at least a survivor. Otherwise, you would not be here reading this book.

Think about those tough times. Some may have become blessings in disguise—the beginning of a completely new and beautiful future.

If you often reflect on your life and express genuine gratitude for overcoming the obstacles in your path, the neural pathways in your brain shift from a defensive state to a prosocial one, reframing your previous traumatic experiences. You become a more optimistic person. Although life will continue to pose challenges, you will have the confidence to look ahead due to your appreciation for past successes in overcoming hardships.

A regular gratitude practice protects you from future challenges in many ways. Anxiety and fear no longer paralyze you. You will have what you need to succeed: a strong motivation and a readiness to overcome obstacles.

BREATHE THANKFULLY

In his popular book, *The Gravity of Gratitude,* Dr. Chandra Shekhar Mayanil recommends a breathing exercise related to thankfulness. This exercise lets the hyperactive mind momentarily pause its constant chatter, relax through deep breathing, and focus on gratitude.

For this activity:

Choose a comfortable place to sit and keep your back straight. If you're sitting in a chair, avoid leaning back against the backrest, as this may hinder your ability to focus on breathing.

Now, close your eyes and become aware of your natural breath flowing in and out. Notice where you feel the breath as it moves in and out – perhaps at the entrance of the nostrils, in the chest as it expands, or in the abdomen as it rises when you breathe in and falls when you breathe out. If your thoughts wander, gently guide them back to the breath. Once you feel calm, begin taking slow, deep breaths, aiming for about four cycles per minute.

Exhale completely.

Breathe in deeply, mentally saying THANK as you breathe in.

Hold for a count of seven.

Silently say " YOU " as you exhale.

Hold for seven counts.

The cycle of breathing in and out forms one complete cycle.

Complete at least seven cycles, which would take about two minutes.

There is no maximum limit to how long you wish to practice.

This exercise enables you to fully engage with the present moment: the NOW.

Buddha's teachings emphasize remaining in the present moment. His approach involves observing the natural breath as it flows in and out.

When I breathe in, I know I'm breathing in.

When I breathe out, I am aware that I'm breathing out.

The past has already passed, and the future is not yet here. The present moment is all that exists. Yet, we waste it by dwelling on the past or worrying about the future. Practising gratitude in the present moment creates harmony in our body and mind.

THANK THE HEALTHY YOU

You may be facing some health concerns.

In health matters, as with other areas of your life, avoid comparing yourself to healthier people. If comparison is necessary, reflect on how much better off you are than those facing more serious health challenges than your own

We often focus on the aspects of our health that need improvement, overlooking all the other areas that have functioned well for us over the years.

If you or someone in your family is facing health issues in any area, take a moment to consider the other healthy aspects for which you can feel grateful:

- I have five essential sense organs: **sight, smell, taste, hearing, and touch**. I am genuinely thankful for everything I can see, hear, smell, taste, and feel.

- Thank you, Universe, for my capable hands granting me independence.

- Thank you, Universe, for my strong **legs** that carry me wherever I wish to go.

- Thank you, Universe, for my healthy **heart** that works tirelessly, 24/7.

- Thank you, universe, for my healthy **lungs,** which give my cells oxygen to revitalize them.

- Thank you, Universe, for my healthy **gut** that digests food and keeps my body nourished.

- Thank you, universe, for my healthy **kidneys** that remove waste from my body.

- Thank you, Universe, for my healthy **liver**, the primary organ that directs my body's digestion.

The list can go on and on....

Here, I will share the *parable of the blind boy*.

A blind boy sat on the sidewalk with an upturned hat at his feet. He held a sign that said, 'I am blind. Please help.'

Many people passed by, but few stopped to drop coins into the hat. A man walking past paused and dropped some coins in the hat. Then, he turned the signboard around and wrote something on it. He placed the board back in the boy's hands so that his writing was visible to passersby.

After a few hours, the man returned, and the hat contained much more money than before. The boy recognized his footsteps as he approached.

The boy asked, "Were you the one who wrote something new on my board this morning? What did you write?"

"I wrote the truth, similar to what you expressed, but in my way. I wrote that **today is a beautiful day, but I cannot see it. "**

Why did this sign attract people to give, while the first one did not? The second sign served as a powerful reminder to be grateful to God for the gift of sight, which this child did not have.

GRATEFUL FOR GIVING

A powerful gratitude practice involves feeling thankful for our ability and capacity to help where needed, whether through monetary support or acts of kindness. Giving creates a sense of purpose and fulfilment, and the gratitude we receive for that assistance is a bonus.

A narrative that expresses gratitude for the opportunity to help.

I want to share an incident involving my friend Joyce.

Joyce was out for her morning walk with a friend when she noticed a couple in front of her slow down. The husband stumbled and fell to the ground.

The two friends rushed forward to help and found him unresponsive, not breathing, and without a pulse. His wife was distraught, shaking him repeatedly in an attempt to elicit a response. Joyce, who had received training in CPR, began performing chest compressions while her friend called for an ambulance. She continued CPR until the ambulance arrived and transported him to the hospital. After a few days, his wife contacted her to express gratitude for saving her husband's life. He had recovered and was discharged from the hospital. Hearing this, tears of happiness filled her eyes. Both husband and wife wanted to meet her personally to thank her. She visited their home and spent time with them. This was a very challenging situation, but the positive aspect was that she could resolve it and discovered two wonderful friends. When Joyce reflects on her feelings about the initial challenge, she expresses joy that she could help to the best of her ability, regardless of the outcome. Learning that she had saved a life filled her with a tremendous sense of gratitude.

Many people know *Mother Teresa*, a missionary nun who dedicated her life to serving the poor, sick, and dying in Kolkata, India. She helped marginalized individuals overlooked by society and expressed gratitude for the chance to assist the sick. She found fulfilment in her work.

Industrialist Andrew Carnegie enjoyed sharing his wealth through philanthropy. He is fondly remembered for his philanthropic legacy.

Bill Gates frequently speaks about how philanthropy, through the Bill and Melinda Gates Foundation, gives him fulfilment and a sense of purpose.

Oskar Schindler, a businessman, used his assets and resources to protect over a thousand Jews from the horrors of the Holocaust during World War II. His reunions with them later in life moved him deeply, and he remained connected with many of them over the years.

Warren Buffett, an American investor and philanthropist, has donated much of his wealth to charitable causes.

Rockefeller, a businessman, enjoyed vitality and longevity after practising philanthropy, which followed his earlier obsession with accumulating wealth.

This does not mean you should only give when you are a billionaire. Whatever we have, whether little or much, can be shared. Offering our time and physical assistance is often more meaningful regarding fulfilment and joy in our personal lives. Let us choose to be grateful, not just for the material things we receive from others but also for the small ways we contribute to their lives.

GRATEFUL FOR RECEIVING THANKS FROM SOMEONE

Dr. Andrew Huberman of the Stanford University School of Medicine asserts that the most potent form of gratitude practice is not merely expressing gratitude but receiving it from someone. However, it is unwise to wait for others to express gratitude toward you constantly.

A similar shift in neurophysiology occurs when you encounter (watch, hear, or read about) a powerful experience of someone else receiving help that emotionally affects you.

He cites several studies conducted in recent years that support this perspective.

There are two kinds of stories that you can use for this practice:

1. Consider a personal experience in which someone expressed gratitude for something you did for them. You remember the emotional impact it had on you.

2. Find a story with special meaning for you - someone who received crucial help at the right moment.

You don't need to recount the entire story each time. Instead, you can jot down bullet point notes on the key aspects:

1. The nature of the struggle.

2. What kind of assistance?

3. How it affected you emotionally

Subsequent story repetitions activated the prosocial neural circuits more efficiently, taking just one or two minutes.

Your personal experience or a compelling story acts as a shortcut to activate the neural circuits of gratitude.

GRATITUDE VISIT

There are several other methods of practising gratitude, including the **Gratitude Visit**. In his TED talk, Martin Seligman discusses the power of the gratitude visit.

If we think back to our past, Many of us can recall someone instrumental in improving our lives. We never thanked this person properly, whether due to circumstances or our unawareness. The person you think about has to be alive.

Now, write a heartfelt testimonial for that person. Call them and express your wish to visit, but don't reveal why.

When you visit and share the testimonial for them to read, it creates an incredibly emotional moment for both of you, fostering lasting happiness even months later. It also helps to rekindle your relationship and bring you closer together.

If you cannot visit this person, you can send them an email or a handwritten letter. Doing so will also make them happy and uplift their mood.

Lastly, let's revisit what we started with at the beginning of the book:

Express gratitude often and sincerely – whether through words or acts of kindness. When we stop taking people for granted and thank them for their tangible gifts or support during difficult times, a new world opens up. You may know the saying that whatever we give to others, the universe rewards us with similar gifts multiplied manifold.

In this regard, I would like to share one final story with you:

The story of Alexander Fleming and Winston Churchill

One day, in the late 19th century, a poor Scottish farmer was working in his fields when he heard a desperate cry for help and rushed toward the sound. He saw a young boy trapped in a bog, struggling for his life. He pulled the boy from the treacherous bog and brought him to safety.

The next day, a wealthy nobleman visited the farmer and introduced himself as Lord Randolph Churchill.

Lord Churchill remarked, "You have saved my son's life. I wish to reward you."

The farmer refused payment, stating that he had acted according to what was right.

The farmer's young son arrived at that moment.

Gazing at him, Lord Churchill said, "If you won't accept money, let me cover your son's education. A bright boy like him deserves a chance."

The farmer accepted the offer. His son attended prestigious schools and subsequently enrolled in medical college. After many years, Lord Churchill's son developed severe pneumonia. At that time, pneumonia was often fatal. However, a new drug that could combat pneumonia was discovered around that period.

Who discovered it? None other than Dr. Alexander Fleming, son of the old Scottish farmer. Lord Churchill's son received treatment with this wonder drug, penicillin, and he recovered. He was Winston Churchill, the future Prime Minister of the United Kingdom.

As you can see, the farmer's kindness is reciprocated by Lord Churchill. Additionally, the Universe rewards Lord Churchill's generosity in educating the farmer's son.

It is easy to start practising gratitude with one or two practices that resonate with us. As our mindset becomes more positive, we will naturally feel inclined to practice gratitude more frequently, leading to a happier life journey.

- **Gratitude Rewires the Brain** – Our brains are wired for survival, focusing on threats rather than happiness. Regular gratitude practice strengthens neural circuits that promote positivity and resilience.

- **Morning Gratitude Practice Sets the Tone** – Expressing gratitude first thing in the morning helps maintain a positive mindset throughout the day. Acknowledge simple blessings like shelter, food, and access to technology.

- **Gratitude Reminders** – Placing visual cues, setting alarms, or associating gratitude with routine actions can help make gratitude a habit. Surrounding yourself with grateful people also reinforces the practice.

- **Journaling Deepens Gratitude** – Writing down blessings and elaborating on them creates a stronger connection to gratitude. Journaling about future aspirations as if they have already happened enhances manifestation.

- **Reflecting on Past Challenges Builds Resilience** – Looking back on difficulties with gratitude for overcoming them promotes optimism and reduces anxiety about future challenges.

- **Mindful Breathing with Gratitude** – A gratitude-focused breathing exercise, such as saying "Thank" while inhaling and "You" while exhaling, brings awareness to the present moment and enhances inner peace.

- **Gratitude for Health Shifts Perspective** – Instead of focusing on ailments, appreciating the healthy parts of the body fosters a sense of well-being and appreciation for physical capabilities.

- **Giving Enhances Gratitude** – Being thankful for the ability to give, whether through acts of kindness or material support, provides a sense of fulfilment and strengthens social connections.

- **Receiving Gratitude is Powerful** – Feeling appreciated by others or witnessing someone receive help can create profound emotional and neurological shifts, reinforcing gratitude.

- **Gratitude Visit Strengthens Relationships** – Expressing appreciation to someone who positively impacted your life, either in person or through a heartfelt letter, fosters deep emotional connections and long-lasting happiness.

Whether you think you can, or you think you can't, you're right

- Henry Ford

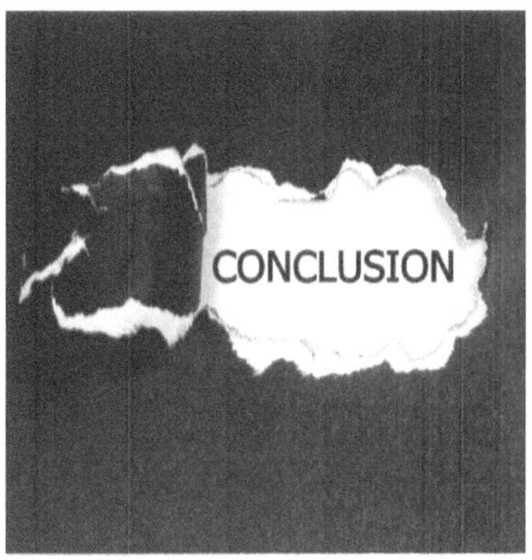

Thank you very much, dear reader, for dedicating your time and effort to reading this book. I hope you found the journey rewarding, that it clarified many of your ideas, and that it helped you discard concepts that no longer align with your current beliefs.

To conclude this book, I would like to refer to Brother David Steindl-Rast. He encourages us to not only have grateful experiences but also to start living gratefully. The present moment is all we truly have. The past is over, and the future is not yet here. If we don't live in the present moment and seize the opportunity it provides, it will slip away, leaving us with nothing.

Br. David proposes a straightforward method to help us start living gratefully:

STOP

LOOK

GO

You can choose what your 'STOP' signs should be. You need something to make you pause in your headlong rush through life. You can place small stickers on the faucet, light switch, mobile phone, laptop, refrigerator door, and countless other items.

Once you pause, you LOOK – observe. Use the amazing sense organs we possess. Be like a child again - open your eyes, ears, and nose, and feel the wonder around you.

Then, 'GO.' Open your heart to the opportunity given to you at this moment. This opportunity may be a way to address your current situation or a chance to help others and bring them joy.

Monitor Your Self-Talk

A powerful concept is that we become what we think about throughout the day. This notion has been attributed to various thinkers and philosophers. It dates back to ancient times when

Marcus Aurelius, a Stoic philosopher, said, "The quality of your life depends on the quality of your thoughts."

Bruce Lee, the martial arts icon, philosopher, and actor, said, "As you think, so shall you become."

Similarly, many philosophers express a unified viewpoint on this issue.

The next time we notice thoughts swirling in our minds, we should pay attention to them. Are they negative or positive?

It is easy to slip into self-pity and a negative mindset filled with ungrateful thoughts about lacking money or resources, missing opportunities, regrets or guilt over past actions, resentment toward someone for not fulfilling your desires, persistent grief over the loss of someone or something dear, complaints about our health issues, bills, waiting in lines, the weather, traffic, inflation, and various individuals, among others. We amplify these ungrateful feelings by expressing them to others. Every time we share our negativity with someone, the threat-responding circuits in our brains become further strengthened.

Recognizing when a negative thought pattern emerges in your mind is crucial. You now understand that negative thoughts can hinder your ability to achieve your goals.

Instead, even if the situation is very upsetting, consider the things you can still be grateful for. This will help you see the problem in perspective rather than feeling overwhelmed.

What Buddha told his disciples thousands of years ago remains relevant today as well:

"Let us rise up and be thankful, for if we didn't learn a lot today, at least we learned a little, and if we didn't learn a little, at least we didn't get sick, and if we got sick, at least we didn't die; so, let us all be thankful."

— Gautama Buddha.

Remember our earlier conversation about the concept of energy frequency? Energy is the basis of everything in the world, including humans, animals, insects, plants, and even inanimate objects.

Instead of allowing low energy frequencies to hold us back, let us all embrace high-frequency emotions such as joy, love, peace, and gratitude. I want to elevate my frequency and experience joy and abundance. What about you?

May you embrace gratitude as a way of life and experience the miraculous blessings of abundance and fulfillment.

BIBLIOGRAPHY

1. David Steindl-Rast – *Anatomy of Gratitude* (January 2016)
   https://www.google.com/search?q=1.+David+Steindl-Rast+%E2%80%93+Anatomy+of+Gratitude+(January+2016)&oq=1.%09David+Steindl-Rast+%E2%80%93+Anatomy+of+Gratitude+(January+2016)&gs_lcrp=EgZjaHJvbWUyBggAEEUYOTIKCAEQABiABBiiBNIBCDMyNzRqMG03qAIAsAIA&sourceid=chrome&ie=UTF-8&sei=2t-Z6PEKOqXseMP44_oiQI#fpstate=ive&vld=cid:abc04986,vid:_KZeRVUIxmA,st:0

2. Robert A. Emmons, *The Little Book of Gratitude* (2016)

3. Summer Allen, University of California, Davis. The white paper titled *"The Science of Gratitude"* was published in 2018.

   https://ggsc.berkeley.edu/images/uploads/GGSC-JTF_White_Paper-Gratitude-FINAL.pdf

4. Emmons, R. A., & McCullough, M. E. (2003). *Counting Blessings Versus Burdens: An Experimental Investigation of Gratitude and Subjective Well-Being in Daily Life.*

5. Priyanka & Prof. Sandeep Singh (2023). ***Effect of Gratitude on Wellbeing: A Systematic Review*. Guru Jambheshwar University of Science and Technology, Hisar, Haryana, India. Published in the** Indian Journal of Psychological Science.

6. Philip C. Watkins, *"Gratitude and the Good Life"* (2013) https://link.springer.com/chapter/10.1007/978-94-007-7253-3_12

7. Andrew Huberman, Stanford University School of Medicine: The Science of Gratitude and How to Build a Gratitude Practice (2022)

   https://www.youtube.com/watch?v=KVjfFN89qvQ&t=4730s

8. Glenn Fox | Brain Science | 2016

   https://www.youtube.com/watch?v=NRNJRInIW8c

9. Shanyan Lei et al. (Jan 2025) Impact of gratitude on post-traumatic growth in patients with coronary stent implantation. National Institutes of Health (NIH) (.gov) https://pmc.ncbi.nlm.nih.gov/articles/PMC11798795/

10. S. Kyeong et al (July 2017) Yonsei University, Seoul, Republic of Korea https://www.researchgate.net/publication/318432721_Effects_of_gratitude_meditation_on_neural_network_functional_connectivity_and_brain-heart_coupling

11. Laura I Hazlett et al. (2021), UCLA - *Exploring neural mechanisms of health benefits of gratitude in women: A randomized controlled trial*

    https://www.sciencedirect.com/science/article/pii/S088915912100177X

12. Fuschia M. Sirois and Alex M. Wood (2017)
https://www.researchgate.net/publication/306356175_Gratitude_Uniquely_Predicts_Lower_Depression_in_Chronic_Illness_Populations_A_Longitudinal_Study_of_Inflammatory_Bowel_Disease_and_Arthritis

13. S B Algoe et al. (2010) It's the little things: Everyday gratitude as a booster shot for romantic relationships (2010)

https://labs.psych.ucsb.edu/gable/shelly/sites/labs.psych.ucsb.edu.gable.shelly/files/pubs/algoe_et_al._2010.pdf

14. A.M. Grant and F. Gino (2010) – A Little Thanks Goes a Long Way: Explaining Why Gratitude Expressions Motivate Prosocial Behavior

https://www.umkc.edu/facultyombuds/documents/grant_gino_jpsp_2010.pdf

15. W.B.Schaufeli, M.B. Leiter, C. Maslach (2009) – Burnout – 35 Years of Research and Practice
https://www.emerald.com/insight/content/doi/10.1108/13620430910966406/full/html?fullSc=1&mbSc=1&fullSc=1

16. Robert A. Emmons – *Thanks! How Practising Gratitude Can Make You Happier* (2007). Harper Collins Publishers

17. Chandra Shekhar Mayanil – *The Gravity of Gratitude* (2023). Notion press.com

18. Martin Seligman - The new era of positive psychology (2004)
https://www.ted.com/talks/martin_seligman_the_new_era_of_positive_psychology?autoplay=true&referrer=playlist-give_thanks

DISCLAIMER

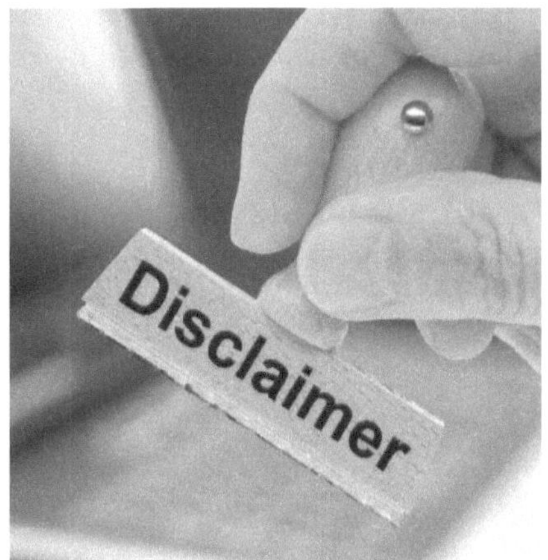

The information provided in this book is for educational and inspirational purposes only. The author has made every effort to ensure accuracy, but this book is not intended as a substitute for professional advice, whether medical, psychological, financial, or otherwise. Readers are encouraged to consult a qualified professional before making any significant changes to their lifestyle, beliefs, or habits based on the content of this book.

The practices and suggestions shared are based on personal experiences, research, and insights into the power of gratitude. Individual results may vary, and the author makes no guarantees regarding specific outcomes.

The author and publisher disclaim any liability for any loss or damage incurred directly or indirectly from the use of the information contained in this book. By reading this book, you acknowledge that you take full responsibility for your actions and interpretations.

Thank you for embarking on this journey of gratitude. May it bring you joy, fulfillment, and a deeper connection with life.

About The Author

Dr. **Kalpana Gupta,** a renowned gynecologist and passionate advocate for holistic healthcare, brings over four decades of experience to her medical practice. She deeply understands the mind-body connection and integrates traditional medicine with complementary therapies to provide comprehensive patient care.

Dr. Gupta's holistic approach focuses on physical healing and addressing the impact of stress, particularly anger and anxiety, on the body's ability to recover.

Beyond her medical practice, Dr. Gupta is actively involved in animal welfare initiatives. Her dedication to the well-being of animals stems from her belief in their profound impact on our lives and the environment.

As a prolific author and dedicated "authorpreneur," Dr. Gupta shares her knowledge and insights through her writings. Her books, articles, and online platforms empower individuals to take charge of their health and embrace a balanced life.

Dr. Gupta's compassionate and relatable writing style makes complex medical concepts accessible to readers from all walks of life.

A Call For Support

Right off the bat, I want to give you a big shout-out for choosing to read my book. You had plenty of other options, but you picked mine, and I really appreciate it. I hope you've gained practical insights to positively impact your everyday life.

Mind sparing me an extra 30 seconds of your time?

I'd absolutely love it if you could leave a review for the book. That would do wonders for expanding my readership and encouraging more folks to give my books a shot.

Just to be clear, reviews are the lifeblood of any author.

It'll only take a minute of your time, but it'll make a world of difference in helping me reach a wider audience. Please leave your review at the store where you purchased the book.

And I'm genuinely excited to read your review. Thanks a ton for your support.